EVERYMAN'S LIBRARY
POCKET POETS

Eat, Drink, and Be Merry

Poems About Food and Drink

Selected and edited by
Peter Washington

EVERYMAN'S LIBRARY

POCKET POETS

Alfred A. Knopf · New York · Toronto

THIS IS A BORZOI BOOK
PUBLISHED BY ALFRED A. KNOPF

This selection by Peter Washington first published in
Everyman's Library, 2003
Copyright © 2003 by Everyman's Library

A list of acknowledgments to copyright owners appears at the back
of this volume.

www.randomhouse.com/everymans

ISBN 1-4000-4023-X

Typography by Peter B. Willberg
Typeset in the UK by AccComputing, North Barrow, Somerset
Printed and bound in Germany by GGP Media, Pössneck

CONTENTS

7

PLAIN FOOD

FOOD

It is always there,
Man's *real* best friend.
It never bites back;
it is already dead.
It never tells us we are lousy lovers
or asks us for an interview.
It simply begs, *Take me*;
it cries out, *I'm yours.*
Mush me all up, it says;
Whatever is you, is pure.

JOHN UPDIKE

UNDUE SIGNIFICANCE

Undue Significance a starving man attaches
To Food –
Far off – He sighs – and therefore – Hopeless –
And therefore – Good –
Partaken – it relieves – indeed –
But proves us
That Spices fly
In the Receipt – It was the Distance –
Was Savory –

EMILY DICKINSON   15

ON FOOD

Alas! What various tastes in food
Divide the human brotherhood!
Birds in their little nests agree
With Chinamen, but not with me.
Colonials like their oysters hot,
Their omelettes heavy – I do not.
The French are fond of slugs and frogs,
The Siamese eat puppy-dogs.
The nobles at the brilliant Court
Of Muscovy consumed a sort
Of candles held and eaten thus,
As though they were asparagus.
The Spaniard, I have heard it said,
Eats garlic, by itself on bread:
Now just suppose a friend or dun
Dropped in to lunch at half-past one
And you were jovially to say,
'Here's bread and garlic! Peg away!'
I doubt if you would gain your end
Or soothe the dun, or please the friend.
In Italy the traveller notes
With great disgust the flesh of goats
Appearing on the table d'hôtes;
And even this the natives spoil
By frying it in rancid oil.

In Maryland they charge like sin
For nasty stuff called terrapin;
And when they ask you out to dine
At Washington, instead of wine,
They give you water from the spring
With lumps of ice for flavouring,
That sometimes kill and always freeze
The high plenipotentiaries.
In Massachusetts all the way
From Boston down to Buzzards Bay
They feed you till you want to die
On rhubarb pie and pumpkin pie,
And horrible huckleberry pie,
And when you summon strength to cry,
'What is there else that I can try?'
They stare at you in mild surprise
And serve you other kinds of pies.
And I with these mine eyes have seen
A dreadful stuff called Margarine
Consumed by men in Bethnal Green.
But I myself that here complain
Confess restriction quite in vain.
I feel my native courage fail
To see a Gascon eat a snail;
I dare not ask abroad for tea;

No cannibal can dine with me;
And all the world is torn and rent
By varying views on nutriment.
And yet upon the other hand,
De gustibus non disputand –

                   – *Um*

HILAIRE BELLOC

TASTE

The body's life with meats and air is fed,
Therefore the soul doth use the tasting power,
In veins which, through the tongue and palate spread,
Distinguish every relish, sweet and sour.

This is the body's nurse; but since man's wit
Found the art of cookery, to delight his sense,
More bodies are consumed and kill'd with it
Than with the sword, famine, or pestilence.

From SATIRES II.2

'Tis yet in vain, I own, to keep a pother
About one Vice, and fall into the other:
Between Excess and Famine lies a mean,
Plain, but not sordid, tho' not splendid, clean.
Avidien or his Wife (no matter which,
For him you'll call a dog, and her a bitch)
Sell their presented Partridges, and Fruits,
And humbly live on rabbits and on roots:
One half-pint bottle serves them both to dine,
And is at once their vinegar and wine.
But on some lucky day (as when they found
A lost Bank-bill, or heard their Son was drown'd)
At such a feast old vinegar to spare,
Is what two souls so gen'rous cannot bear;
Oyl, tho' it stink, they drop by drop impart,
But sowse the Cabbidge with a bounteous heart.

He knows to live, who keeps the middle state,
And neither leans on this side, nor on that:
Nor stops, for one bad Cork, his Butler's pay,
Swears, like Albutius, a good Cook away;
Nor lets, like Nævius, ev'ry error pass,
The musty wine, foul cloth, or greasy glass.

Now hear what blessings Temperance can bring:
(Thus said our Friend, and what he said I sing.)
First Health: The stomach (cram'd from ev'ry dish,

A Tomb of boil'd, and roast, and flesh, and fish,
Where Bile, and wind, and phlegm, and acid jar,
And all the Man is one intestine war)
Remembers oft the School-boy's simple fare,
The temp'rate sleeps, and spirits light as air!
   How pale, each Worshipful and rev'rend Guest
Rise from a Clergy, or a City, feast!
What life in all that ample Body say,
What heav'nly Particle inspires the clay?
The Soul subsides; and wickedly inclines
To seem but mortal, ev'n in sound Divines.
On morning wings how active springs the Mind,
That leaves the load of yesterday behind?
How easy ev'ry labour it pursues?
How coming to the Poet ev'ry Muse?
Not but we may exceed, some Holy time,
Or tir'd in search of Truth, or search of Rhyme.
Ill Health some just indulgence may engage,
And more, the Sickness of long Life, Old-age:
For fainting Age what cordial drop remains,
If our intemp'rate Youth the Vessel drains?

A GLASS OF WATER

Here is a glass of water from my well.
It tastes of rock and root and earth and rain;
It is the best I have, my only spell,
And it is cold, and better than champagne.
Perhaps someone will pass this house one day
To drink, and be restored, and go his way,
Someone in dark confusion as I was
When I drank down cold water in a glass,
Drank a transparent health to keep me sane,
After the bitter mood had gone again.

BREAD

Hunger was loneliness, betrayed
By the pitiless candour of the stars'
Talk, in an old byre he prayed

Not for food; to pray was to know
Waking from a dark dream to find
The white loaf on the white snow;

Not for warmth, warmth brought the rain's
Blurring of the essential point
Of ice probing his raw pain.

He prayed for love, love that would share
His rags' secret; rising he broke
Like sun crumbling the gold air

The live bread for the starved folk.

MILK, MILK, MILK

This picture may seem
To you, when first you spy it,
An outdoor hareem
Of ladies running riot,
But such is not the case,
So don't be too inquiet,
We're here
Because we're mere-
Ly on a diet.
And what a diet!
Oh, for some Colony mayonnaise,
Oh, for a Plaza demitasse,
Oh, to be back
With Charlie and Jack
In those plush rooms,
Eating mushrooms
Under glass!
Oh, for some broccoli Hollandaise
And those other dear dishes of that
ilk.
This cure, so they state,
Will make a girl reduce her weight,
But, brudder,
Why flood 'er
With milk?

Milk – at eight o'clock,
Milk – at ten o'clock,
Noon – and then a clock
Strikes – and we get some more
    milk,
Milk – at two o'clock,
Milk – at four o'clock,
Six – once more a clock
Strikes – and we get some more
    milk,
And what do you think
They give us to drink
When we settle in our sheets of
    silk?
Milk, milk, milk, milk,
Big bumpers of milk!

OF TEA, COMMENDED BY HER MAJESTY

Venus her myrtle, Phœbus has his bays;
Tea both excels, which she vouchsafes to praise.
The best of queens, and best of herbs, we owe
To that bold nation which the way did show
To the fair region where the sun does rise,
Whose rich productions we so justly prize.
The Muse's friend, tea does our fancy aid,
Repress those vapours which the head invade,
And keeps that palace of the soul serene,
Fit on her birth-day to salute the Queen.

EDMUND WALLER

THE TWO TEAPOTS

The small teapot to the large teapot,
Stewed as a pond: 'When you last spoke,
Chuckling generously from your girth and glaze,
There were many who listened, who were friends.
Where are they now?'

The large teapot to the small teapot,
Clogged to a trickle: 'Peace, brother,
Your words are still warm and waited for
By one who will be loved, though alone.
Be contented.'

COFFEE

Coffee arrives, that grave and wholesome Liquor,
That heals the stomach, makes the genius quicker,
Relieves the memory, revives the sad,
And cheers the Spirits, without making mad...

ANON.

From THE RAPE OF THE LOCK

For lo! The Board with Cups and Spoons is crown'd,
The Berries crackle, and the Mill turns round.
On shining Altars of *Japan* they raise
The silver Lamp; the fiery Spirits blaze.
From silver Spouts the grateful Liquors glide,
While *China*'s Earth receives the smoking Tyde.
At once they gratify their Scent and Taste,
And frequent Cups prolong the rich Repast...
Coffee, (which makes the Politician wise,
And see thro' all things with his half-shut eyes...)

ALEXANDER POPE   27

FARM WIFE

Hers is the clean apron, good for fire
Or lamp to embroider, as we talk slowly
In the long kitchen, while the white dough
Turns to pastry in the great oven,
Sweetly and surely as hay making
In a June meadow; hers are the hands,
Humble with milking, but still now
In her wide lap as though they heard
A quiet music, hers being the voice
That coaxes time back to the shadows
In the room's corners. O, hers is all
This strong body, the safe island
Where men may come, sons and lovers,
Daring the cold seas of her eyes.

SQUARE MEALS

SUNDAY MORNING BREAKFAST TIME

Here's to the piping porridge,
Here's to the biscuits hot,
Here's to the java
Flowing like lava
Out of the coffee pot.
Here's to the eggs and bacon,
Here's to the waffles unique,
And here's and here's
Three rousing cheers
For the best meal of the week!

For it's Sunday morning breakfast time,
The time all men adore!
Why don't the poets go into rhyme
And rave about it more?
For only then can a man forget
The sweat and the worries of his bane-
Ful lot as he calmly enjoys his toast
And most of Arthur Brisbane.
Breakfast time on other days
Means bolting at fever heat,
But on Sunday morning, there's the time
When a man has time to eat – and eat,
When a man has time to . . .
[*Cakewalk*]
. . . Breakfast is served.

COLE PORTER   31

DR BROWNING AT BREAKFAST

'Will ye take a scrambled egg, Dr Browning, with your
    toast,
  Or p'raps the daintiest slice of ham or beef,
Or a snack of Finnan haddie (and ye'll pardon me
    the boast)
  O' dainties they Scots haddies are the chief;
There's porritch on the wagon, Dr Browning,
    if ye wish,
  And devilled kidneys comin' from below
And if ye'd wet your whistle – o' coky take a dish –'
  'Cocoa! Mrs Green, Cocoa!'

'Anchovies are beside ye and honey from the hive,
  And creases if ye'd like a bit o' green;
Or just look'ee at that lobster – in the pot at half
    past five;
  Or if it takes your fancy a sardine.
If furrin is your taste there's some Rooshan caviare
  Or them apricocks that Green himself did grow
La, and if ye'd wet your whistle there's coky, and
    to spare –'
  'Cocoa!! Mrs Green, Cocoa!!'

'Have a mushroom or a muffin, all a-swimming in
      its grease
   Or a slice of brawn, a relishin' o' mace;
Just make yeself at 'ome, Dr Browning, if ye please,
   I would like to see ye plumper in the face.
Grilled trout and seedy cake, peach preserve and
      prawns in pots
Fried sassage, bacon, ox tongue, and cod's roe,
Why, and if ye'd wet your whistle there's coky
      pipin' hot –'
   'Cocoa!!! Mrs Green, Cocoa!!!'

A MIRACLE FOR BREAKFAST

At six o'clock we were waiting for coffee,
waiting for coffee and the charitable crumb
that was going to be served from a certain balcony,
– like kings of old, or like a miracle.
It was still dark. One foot of the sun
steadied itself on a long ripple in the river.

The first ferry of the day had just crossed the river.
It was so cold we hoped that the coffee
would be very hot, seeing that the sun
was not going to warm us; and that the crumb
would be a loaf each, buttered, by a miracle.
At seven a man stepped out on the balcony.

He stood for a minute alone on the balcony
looking over our heads toward the river.
A servant handed him the makings of a miracle,
consisting of one lone cup of coffee
and one roll, which he proceeded to crumb,
his head, so to speak, in the clouds – along with
    the sun.

Was the man crazy? What under the sun
was he trying to do, up there on his balcony!
Each man received one rather hard crumb,

which some flicked scornfully into the river,
and, in a cup, one drop of the coffee.
Some of us stood around, waiting for the miracle.

I can tell what I saw next; it was not a miracle.
A beautiful villa stood in the sun
and from its doors came the smell of hot coffee.
In front, a baroque white plaster balcony
added by birds, who nest along the river,
– I saw it with one eye close to the crumb –

and galleries and marble chambers. My crumb
my mansion, made for me by a miracle,
through ages, by insects, birds, and the river
working the stone. Every day, in the sun,
at breakfast time I sit on my balcony
with my feet up, and drink gallons of coffee.

We licked up the crumb and swallowed the coffee.
A window across the river caught the sun
as if the miracle were working, on the wrong balcony.

'I NEVER HAD A PIECE OF TOAST'

I never had a piece of toast,
    Particularly long and wide,
But fell upon the sanded floor;
    And always on the buttered side.

ANON., AFTER THOMAS MOORE

BREAKFAST

Twenty sparrows
on

a scattered
turd:

Share and share
alike.

BREAKFAST WITH
GERARD MANLEY HOPKINS

*Delicious heart-of-the-corn, fresh-from-the-oven flakes are
sparkled and spangled with sugar for a can't-be-resisted
flavour.*
         Legend on a packet of breakfast cereal

Serious over my cereals I broke one breakfast my fast
   With something-to-read-searching retinas retained
     by print on a packet;
Sprung rhythm sprang, and I found (the mind fact-
     mining at last)
   An influence Father-Hopkins-fathered on the
     copywriting racket.
Parenthesis-proud, bracket-bold, happiest with
     hyphens,
   The writers stagger intoxicated by terms, adjective-
     unsteadied –
Describing in graceless phrases fizzling like soda
     siphons
   All things crisp, crunchy, malted, tangy, sugared
     and shredded.
Far too, yes, too early we are urged to be purged,
     to savour
   Salt, malt and phosphates in English twisted and
     torn,

As, sparkled and spangled with sugar for a can't-be-
    resisted flavour
  Come fresh-from-the-oven flakes direct from the
    heart of the corn.

ANTHONY BRODE

EPIGRAM III.27

Our dinner invitations are one-sided:
When I ask you, you usually come; yet you
Never ask me. I shouldn't mind, provided
You asked nobody else. However, you do.
Neither one of us, Gallus, comes out blameless.
What do I mean? I'm stupid and you're shameless.

EPIGRAM X.48

Two o'clock: the Egyptian priests have barred
   the temple gates, the Palace troop changed guard.
The baths are cooler now, that still breathed steam
   at one, and noon seemed hot as Nero's stream.
Cerialis, Stella, Canius, Flaccus, Nepos –
   with you we're six – my couch holds sev'n: add Lupus.
Okra (that purges) by my good dame got,
   expect, with riches from my garden plot.
Mint there'll be (for wind), leeks in slices,
   short-head lettuce, rocket (for what's nice is).
Scad, dressed with devilled eggs & sprigs of rue,
   sows' teats well sprinkled with a tunny stew.
These for tasters: the meal itself – one course,
   a kid made tender in some wild beast's jaws,
With morselled meats so carving is left out,
   & builders' beans & tender cabbage sprouts.
A chicken & a thrice-left-over ham
   as well. When filled, you've fruit & Nomentan –
Decanted from the flagon with no dreg,
   (Frontinus consul) three years in the keg.
And add to this, the jest that does not bite,
   a lack of fear of what you did last night,
Or said. Talk Green & Blue – the Circus show . . .
   None from my Nomentan shall bad-mouthed go.

AFTER LUNCH

After lunch – one short nap;
On waking up – two cups of tea.
Raising my head, I see the sun's light
Once again slanting to the south-west.
Those who are happy regret the shortness of the day;
Those who are sad tire of the year's sloth.
But those whose hearts are devoid of joy or sadness
Just go on living, regardless of 'short' or 'long'.

PO CHU-I
TRANS. ARTHUR WALEY

TEA

When the elephant's-ear in the park
Shrivelled in frost,
And the leaves on the paths
Ran like rats,
Your lamp-light fell
On shining pillows,
Of sea-shades and sky-shades,
Like umbrellas in Java.

THE BANQUET

A gathering of good friends
talking quietly outdoors,

the banquet being served, a dry rosé
with a bite of kebab afterwards,

a wink from the one who pours,
Hafiz telling some story,

Hajji Qavam with his long laugh,
a full moon overhead,

the infinite mystery
of all this love.

If someone doesn't want the pleasure
of such an openhearted garden,

companionship, no, life itself,
must be against his rules!

ANGELO ORDERS HIS DINNER

I, Angelo, obese, black-garmented,
Respectable, much in demand, well fed
With mine own larder's dainties, – where, indeed,
Such cakes of myrrh or fine alyssum seed,
Thin as a mallow-leaf, embrowned o' the top,
Which, cracking, lets the ropy, trickling drop
Of sweetness touch your tongue, or potted nests
Which my recondite recipe invests
With cold conglomerate tidbits – ah, the bill!
(You say,) but given it were mine to fill
My chests, the case so put were yours, we'll say,
(This counter, here, your post, as mine to-day,)
And you've an eye to luxuries, what harm
In smoothing down your palate with the charm
Yourself concocted? There we issue take;
And see! as thus across the rim I break
This puffy paunch of glazed embroidered cake,
So breaks, through use, the lust of watering chaps
And craveth plainness: do I so? Perhaps;
But that's my secret. Find me such a man
As Lippo yonder, built upon the plan
Of heavy storage, double-navelled, fat
From his own giblets' oil, an Ararat
Uplift o'er water, sucking rosy draughts
From Noah's vineyard, – ... crisp, enticing wafts

Yon kitchen now emits, which to your sense
Somewhat abate the fear of old events,
Qualms to the stomach, – I, you see, am slow
Unnecessary duties to forgo, –
You understand? A venison haunch, *haut goût*,
Ducks that in Cimbrian olives mildly stew,
And sprigs of anise, might one's teeth provoke
To taste, and so we wear the complex yoke
Just as it suits, – my liking, I confess,
More to receive, and to partake no less,
Still more obese, while through thick adipose
Sensation shoots, from testing tongue to toes
Far-off, dim-conscious, at the body's verge,
Where the froth-whispers of its waves emerge
On the untasting sand. Stay, now! a seat
Is bare: I, Angelo, will sit and eat.

LE DÎNER

Come along, 'tis the time, ten or more minutes past,
And he who came first had to wait for the last;
The oysters ere this had been in and been out;
Whilst I have been sitting and thinking about
   How pleasant it is to have money, heigh-ho!
   How pleasant it is to have money.

A clear soup with eggs; *voilà tout*; of the fish
The *filets de sole* are a moderate dish
A la Orly, but you're for red mullet, you say:
By the gods of good fare, who can question to-day
   How pleasant it is to have money, heigh-ho!
   How pleasant it is to have money.

After oysters, sauterne; then sherry; champagne,
Ere one bottle goes, comes another again;
Fly up, thou bold cork, to the ceiling above,
And tell to our ears in the sound that they love
   How pleasant it is to have money, heigh-ho!
   How pleasant it is to have money.

I've the simplest of palates; absurd it may be,
But I almost could dine on a *poulet-au-riz*,
Fish and soup and omelette and that – but the deuce –
There were to be woodcocks, and not *Charlotte Russe*.

So pleasant it is to have money, heigh-ho!
So pleasant it is to have money.

Your Chablis is acid, away with the Hock,
Give me the pure juice of the purple Médoc:
St Peray is exquisite; but, if you please,
Some Burgundy just before tasting the cheese.
    So pleasant it is to have money, heigh-ho!
    So pleasant it is to have money.

As for that, pass the bottle, and d——n the expense,
I've seen it observed by a writer of sense,
That the labouring classes could scarce live a day,
If people like us didn't eat, drink, and pay.
    So useful it is to have money, heigh-ho!
    So useful it is to have money.

One ought to be grateful, I quite apprehend,
Having dinner and supper and plenty to spend,
And so suppose now, while the things go away,
By way of a grace we all stand up and say
    How pleasant it is to have money, heigh-ho!
    How pleasant it is to have money.

A. H. CLOUGH

A LITERARY DINNER

Come here, said my hostess, her face making room
for one of those pink introductory smiles
that link, like a valley of fruit trees in bloom,
the slopes of two names.
I want you, she murmured, to eat Dr James.

I was hungry. The Doctor looked good. He had read
the great book of the week and had liked it, he said,
because it was powerful. So I was brought
a generous helping. His mauve-bosomed wife
kept showing me, very politely, I thought,
the tenderest bits with the point of her knife.
I ate – and in Egypt the sunsets were swell;
The Russians were doing remarkably well;
had I met a Prince Poprinsky, whom he had known
in Caparabella, or was it Mentone?
They had traveled extensively, he and his wife;
her hobby was People, his hobby was Life.
All was good and well cooked, but the tastiest part
was his nut-flavored, crisp cerebellum. The heart
resembled a shiny brown date,
and I stowed all the studs on the edge of my plate.

INVITING A FRIEND TO SUPPER

Tonight, grave sir, both my poor house, and I
    Do equally desire your company:
Not that we think us worthy such a guest,
    But that your worth will dignify our feast,
With those that come; whose grace may make
        that seem
    Something, which, else, could hope for no esteem.
It is the fair acceptance, sir, creates
    The entertainment perfect: not the cates.
Yet shall you have, to rectify your palate,
    An olive, capers, or some better salad
Ush'ring the mutton; with a short-legged hen,
    If we can get her, full of eggs, and then,
Lemons, and wine for sauce: to these, a cony
    Is not to be despaired of, for our money;
And, though fowl, now, be scarce, yet there are clerks,
    The sky not falling, think we may have larks.
I'll tell you of more, and lie, so you will come:
    Of partridge, pheasant, woodcock, of which some
May yet be there; and godwit, if we can:
    Knat, rail, and ruff too. Howsoe'er, my man
Shall read a piece of Virgil, Tacitus,
    Livy, or of some better book to us,
Of which we'll speak our minds, amidst our meat;
    And I'll profess no verses to repeat:

To this, if aught appear, which I not know of,
    That will the pastry, not my paper, show of.
Digestive cheese, and fruit there sure will be;
    But that, which most doth take my muse, and me,
Is a pure cup of rich canary wine,
    Which is the Mermaid's, now, but shall be mine:
Of which had Horace, or Anacreon tasted,
    Their lives, as do their lines, till now had lasted.
Tobacco, nectar, or the Thespian spring,
    Are all but Luther's beer, to this I sing.
Of this we will sup free, but moderately,
    And we will have no Poley, or Parrot by;
Nor shall our cups make any guilty men:
    But, at our parting, we will be, as when
We innocently met. No simple word,
    That shall be uttered at our mirthful board,
Shall make us sad next morning: or affright
    The liberty, that we'll enjoy tonight.

SUPPER WITH LINDSAY

I deal in wisdom, not in dry desire.
Luck! Luck! that's what I care for in a cage
And what fool wouldn't, when things from sleep
Come easy to the sill, things lost from far away.
Behold, the Moon! –
And it stepped in the room, under his arm, –
Lindsay's I mean: two moons, or even three,
I'd say my face is just as round as his,
And that makes three, counting his face as one.
'What Moon?' he cried, half-turning in mock fury.

And then it spilled:
The sudden light spilled on the floor like cream
From a knocked over churn, and foamed around
Us, under the chair-rungs, toward the cellar door.

'Let's eat!' said Lindsay. 'Here we've got the Moon,
We've got the living light, but where's the food?'

'Sure, we still eat,' I said. 'Enough! Or too much.'
– 'That means Blake, too?'

                           When Lindsay bent his head
Half sideways in the shifting light,
His nose looked even bigger than it was,

And one eye gazed askew. 'Why, Blake, he's dead, –
But come to think, they say the same of me.'

When he said that, a spidery shape dropped down
A swaying light-cord, then ran half-way back.

'That's never Blake,' said Lindsay. 'He'd be a worm,
One of those fat ones winding through a rose.
Maybe it's Whitman's spider, I can't tell,
Let's eat before the moonlight all runs out.'

So we sat down and ate ourselves a meal,
But what we ate I can't remember quite:
Cornbread and milk, ice cream and more ice cream,
With cold roast beef and coffee for dessert –
Mostly I remember the ice cream.

After a while the light began to wane
And flicker near our legs like kerosene
Burning in sand. 'It looks like I should go,' –
And Lindsay heaved himself from my old chair.
'The spider's gone,' he said bemusedly.

'Who called me poet of the college yell?
We need a breed that mixes Blake and me,
Heroes and bears, and old philosophers –
John Ransom should be here, and René Char;

Paul Bunyan is part Russian, did you know? –
We're getting closer to it all the time.'

I walked him through the grill and out the gate
Past alder lane, and we gabbed there a while.
He shook my hand. 'Tell Williams I've been here,
And Robert Frost. They might remember me.'

With that, he hitched his pants and humped away.

POETRY FOR SUPPER

'Listen, now, verse should be as natural
As the small tuber that feeds on muck
And grows slowly from obtuse soil
To the white flower of immortal beauty.'

'Natural, hell! What was it Chaucer
Said once about the long toil
That goes like blood to the poem's making?
Leave it to nature and the verse sprawls,
Limp as bindweed, if it break at all
Life's iron crust. Man, you must sweat
And rhyme your guts taut, if you'd build
Your verse a ladder.'
                                'You speak as though
No sunlight ever surprised the mind
Groping on its cloudy path.'

'Sunlight's a thing that needs a window
Before it enter a dark room.
Windows don't happen.'
                                So two old poets,
Hunched at their beer in the low haze
Of an inn parlour, while the talk ran
Noisily by them, glib with prose.

SOMETHING ON A TRAY

Advancing years may bring about
A rather sweet nostalgia
In spite of rheumatism and gout
And, certainly, neuralgia.
And so, when we have churned our way
Through luncheon and a matinée,
We gratefully to bed retire
Obsessed with an acute desire
To rest our aching, creaking vertebrae
And have a little something on a tray.

Some ageing ladies with a groan
Renounce all beauty lotions,
They dab their brows with eau-de-Cologne
And turn to their devotions,
We face the process of decay
Attired in a négligé
And with hot bottles at our toes
We cosily in bed repose
Enjoying, in a rather languid way,
A little 'eggy' something on a tray.

Advancing years that many dread
Still have their compensations,
We turn when youth and passion have fled

To more sedate sensations,
And when we've fought our weary way
Through some exhausting social day
We thankfully to bed retire
With pleasant book and crackling fire
And, like Salome in a bygone day,
Enjoy a little something on a tray.

When weary from the fray
Something on a tray
Sends weariness away,
Something on a tray,
Thank God, thank God we say,
For something on a tray.

THE HEVER PICNIC

Shock howled: the merry buzz stopped dead;
All but Anne went terrified,
As round the bush at a tall man's stride
    Came Luckie Lee,
     Queen of the Egyptians.

Anne, cutting her a slice of pound-cake, said:
'Why d'you stare so – what d'you see!
'Staring like a hawk at me,
'Good woman?'
     'H'm', their guest replied,
'Weddings . . . beddings . . . and . . .'
         'And what?'
The lovely Bullen begged.
        'And that
'Is all, as far as I can see',
And – muttering to herself aside:
'Not for both her silver bracelets' –
Round the bush at twice the stride
    Went Luckie Lee,
     Queen of the Egyptians.

THE DINING ROOM

A room with low windows, with brown shades,
Where a Danzig clock keeps silent in the corner;
A low leather sofa; and right above it
The sculpted heads of two smiling devils;
And a copper pan shows its gleaming paunch.

On the wall, a painting that depicts winter.
A crowd of people skate on ice
Between the trees, smoke comes from a chimney,
And crows fly in an overcast sky.

Nearby a second clock. A bird sits inside.
It pops out squawking and calls three times.
And it has barely finished its third and last call
When mother ladles out soup from a hot tureen.

RESTAURANT CAR

Fondling only to throttle the nuzzling moment
Smuggled under the table, hungry or not
We roughride over the sleepers, finger the menu,
Avoid our neighbours' eyes and wonder what

Mad country moves beyond the steamed-up window
So fast into the past we could not keep
Our feet on it one instant. Soup or grapefruit?
We had better eat to pass the time, then sleep

To pass the time. The water in the carafe
Shakes its hips, both glass and soup plate spill,
The tomtom beats in the skull, the waiters totter
Along their invisible tightrope. For good or ill.

For fish or meat, with single tickets only,
Our journey still in the nature of a surprise,
Could we, before we stop where all must change,
Take one first risk and catch our neighbours' eyes?

FRUIT

THE FRUIT

It climbed and climbed from earth invisibly,
and kept its secret in the silent stem,
and turned in the clear blossom into flame,
and then resumed its secrecy.

And through a whole long summer fructified
within that day and night travailing tree,
and felt itself as urging instancy
to meet responding space outside.

And though it now displays so shiningly
that rondure of completed rest anew,
within the rind it sinks resigningly
back to the centre it outgrew.

THE DISH OF FRUIT

The table describes
nothing: four legs, by which
it becomes a table. Four lines
by which it becomes a quatrain,

the poem that lifts the dish
of fruit, if we say it is like
a table – how will it describe
the contents of the poem?

WILLIAM CARLOS WILLIAMS

FORBIDDEN FRUIT

Forbidden Fruit a flavor has
That lawful Orchards mocks –
How luscious lies within the Pod
The Pea that Duty locks –

KELMSCOTT CRAB APPLES

Fair is the world, now autumn's wearing,
And the sluggard sun lies long abed;
Sweet are the days, now winter's nearing,
And all winds feign that the wind is dead.

Dumb is the hedge where the crabs hang yellow,
Bright as the blossoms of the spring;
Dumb is the close where the pears grow mellow,
And none but the dauntless redbreasts sing.

Fair was the spring, but amidst his greening
Grey were the days of the hidden sun;
Fair was the summer, but overweening,
So soon his o'er-sweet days were done.

Come then, love, for peace is upon us.
Far off is failing, and far is fear,
Here where the rest in the end hath won us,
In the garnering tide of the happy year.

Come from the grey old house by the water,
Where, far from the lips of the hungry sea,
Green groweth the grass o'er the field of the slaughter,
And all is a tale for thee and me.

WILLIAM MORRIS   63

APPLES FOR PAUL SUTTMAN

Chardin, Cézanne, they had their apples,
    As did Paris and Eve –
Sleek, buxom pippins with inverted nipples;
    And surely we believe

That Pluto has his own unsweet earth apples
    Blooming among the dead,
There in the thick of Radamanthine opals,
    Blake's hand, Bernini's head.

Ours are not golden overtures to trouble
    Or molds of fatal choice,
But like some fleshed epitome, the apple
    Entreats us to rejoice

In more than flavor, nourishment, or color,
    Or jack or calvados;
Nor are we rendered, through ingested dolor,
    Sinful or comatose.

It speaks to us quite otherwise, in supple
    Convexity and ply,
Smooth, modeled slopes, familiar rills. Crab apple,
    Winesap and Northern Spy

Tell us Hogarth's 'Analysis of Beauty'
    Or architect's French Curve
Cannot proclaim what Aphrodite's putti
    Both celebrate and serve:

Those known hyperbolas, those rounds and gradients,
    Dingle and shadowed dip,
The commonwealth of joy, imagined radiance,
    Thoughts of that faultless lip.

The dearest curves in nature – the merest ripple,
    The cresting wave – release
All of our love, and find it in an apple,
    My Helen, your Elisse.

MOONLIT APPLES

At the top of the house the apples are laid in rows,
And the skylight lets the moonlight in, and those
Apples are deep-sea apples of green. There goes
   A cloud on the moon in the autumn light.
A mouse in the wainscot scratches, and scratches,
     and then
There is no sound at the top of the house of men
Or mice; and the cloud is blown, and the moon again
   Dapples the apples with deep-sea light.
They are lying in rows there, under the gloomy beams;
On the sagging floor; they gather the silver streams
Out of the moon, those moonlit apples of dreams,
   And quiet is the steep stair under.
In the corridors under there is nothing but sleep.
And stiller than ever on orchard boughs they keep
Tryst with the moon, and deep is the silence, deep
   On moon-washed apples of wonder.

QUINCE

It is yellow in colour, as if it wore a daffodil
tunic, and it smells like musk, a penetrating smell.

It has the perfume of a loved woman and the same
hardness of heart, but it has the colour of the
impassioned and scrawny lover.

Its pallor is borrowed from my pallor; its smell
is my sweetheart's breath.

When it stood fragrant on the bough and the leaves
had woven for it a covering of brocade,

I gently put up my hand to pluck it and to set it
like a censer in the middle of my room.

It had a cloak of ash-coloured down hovering over
its smooth golden body,

and when it lay naked in my hand, with nothing
        more than
its daffodil-coloured shift,

it made me think of her I cannot mention, and I feared
the ardour of my breath would shrivel it in my fingers.

Isn't that Aphrodite's apple?

SHAFER BEN UTMAN AL-MUSHAFI   67
TRANS. A. L. LLOYD

A QUINCE PRESERVED THROUGH THE WINTER, GIVEN TO A LADY

I'm a quince, saved over from last year, still fresh,
   my skin young, not spotted or wrinkled, downy as
     the new-born,
as though I were still among my leaves. Seldom
   does winter yield such gifts, but for you, my queen,
even the snows and frosts bear harvests like this.

ANTIPHILOS
TRANS. W. S. MERWIN

THE LEMON

And the lemon on its branch is true gold;
A coloured ball which once struck hangs in flight
For an eye blink, still poised on the swung polo stick.

68   ABDULLAH IBN AL-MU'TAZZ
     TRANS. G. B. H. WIGHTMAN AND
     ABDULLAH AL-UDHARI

THE STRAWBERRY PLANT

Above the water, in her rocky niche,
She sat enthroned and perfect; for her crown
One bud like pearl, and then two fairy roses
Blanched and yet ardent in their glowing hearts:
One greenish berry spangling into yellow
Where the light touched the seed: one fruit achieved
And ripe, an odorous vermilion ball
Tight with completion, lovingly enclasped
By the close cup whose green chimed with the red,
And showered with drops of gold like Danaë:
Three lovely sister leaves as like as peas,
Young but full-fledged, dark, with a little down:
Two leaves that to a matron hue inclined;
And one the matriarch, that dressed in gold
And flushed with wine, thought her last days her best.
And here and there a diamond of dew
Beamed coolly from the white, smiled from the gold,
Silvered the down, struck lightning from the red.
The overhanging rock forbade the sun,
Yet she was all alight with water-gleams
Reflected, like the footlights at a play:
Perfection's self, and (rightly) out of reach.

NEVERTHELESS

you've seen a strawberry
    that's had a struggle; yet
    was, where the fragments met,

a hedgehog or a star-
    fish for the multitude
    of seeds. What better food

than apple seeds – the fruit
    within the fruit – locked in
    like counter-curved twin

hazelnuts? Frost that kills
    the little rubber-plant-
    leaves of *kok-saghyz*-stalks, can't

harm the roots; they still grow
    in frozen ground. Once where
    there was a prickly-pear-

leaf clinging to barbed wire,
    a root shot down to grow
    in earth two feet below;

as carrots form mandrakes
    or a ram's-horn root some-
    times. Victory won't come

to me unless I go
    to it; a grape tendril
    ties a knot in knots till

knotted thirty times – so
    the bound twig that's under-
    gone and over-gone, can't stir.

The weak overcomes its
    menace, the strong over-
    comes itself. What is there

like fortitude! What sap
    went through that little thread
    to make the cherry red!

PERSIMMONS

Wild persimmons
The mother eating
The bitter part.

ISSA
TRANS. ANON.

THE CLOUD-BERRY

Around me cluster quaint cloud-berry flowers,
That love the moist slopes of the highest tops,
Pale white, and delicate, and beautiful,
Yet lowly growing 'mid the black peat moss, –
No life with darker root and fairer bloom:
As if the hand of God had secret wrought
Amid the peaty chaos and decay
Of long deep buried years, and from the moss
Entombed, unshaped, unsunned, and colourless,
Set free a form of beauty rare and bright,
To typify the glory and the grace
Which from the dust of death He will awake,
In course of time, on Resurrection morn!

BLUEBERRIES

'You ought to have seen what I saw on my way
To the village, through Patterson's pasture today:
Blueberries as big as the end of your thumb,
Real sky-blue, and heavy, and ready to drum
In the cavernous pail of the first one to come!
And all ripe together, not some of them green
And some of them ripe! You ought to have seen!'

'I don't know what part of the pasture you mean.'

'You know where they cut off the woods – let me see –
It was two years ago – or no! – can it be
No longer than that? – and the following fall
The fire ran and burned it all up but the wall.'

'Why, there hasn't been time for the bushes to grow.
That's always the way with the blueberries, though:
There may not have been the ghost of a sign
Of them anywhere under the shade of the pine,
But get the pine out of the way, you may burn
The pasture all over until not a fern
Or grass-blade is left, not to mention a stick,
And presto, they're up all around you as thick
And hard to explain as a conjuror's trick.'

'It must be on charcoal they fatten their fruit.
I taste in them sometimes the flavor of soot.
And after all, really they're ebony skinned:
The blue's but a mist from the breath of the wind,
A tarnish that goes at a touch of the hand,
And less than the tan with which pickers are tanned.'

'Does Patterson know what he has, do you think?'

'He may and not care, and so leave the chewink
To gather them for him – you know what he is.
He won't make the fact that they're rightfully his
An excuse for keeping us other folk out.'

'I wonder you didn't see Loren about.'

'The best of it was that I did. Do you know,
I was just getting through what the field had to show
And over the wall and into the road,
When who should come by, with a democrat-load
Of all the young chattering Lorens alive,
But Loren, the fatherly, out for a drive.'

'He saw you, then? What did he do? Did he frown?'

'He just kept nodding his head up and down.
You know how politely he always goes by.
But he thought a big thought – I could tell by his eye –
Which being expressed, might be this in effect:
"I have left those there berries, I shrewdly suspect,
To ripen too long. I am greatly to blame." '

'He's a thriftier person than some I could name.'

'He seems to be thrifty; and hasn't he need,
With the mouths of all those young Lorens to feed?
He has brought them all up on wild berries, they say,
Like birds. They store a great many away.
They eat them the year round, and those they don't eat
They sell in the store and buy shoes for their feet.'

'Who cares what they say? It's a nice way to live,
Just taking what Nature is willing to give,
Not forcing her hand with harrow and plow.'

'I wish you had seen his perpetual bow –
And the air of the youngsters! Not one of them turned,
And they looked so solemn-absurdly concerned.'

'I wish I knew half what the flock of them know
Of where all the berries and other things grow,
Cranberries in bogs and raspberries on top

Of the boulder-strewn mountain, and when they
    will crop.
I met them one day and each had a flower
Stuck into his berries as fresh as a shower;
Some strange kind – they told me it hadn't a name.'

'I've told you how once, not long after we came,
I almost provoked poor Loren to mirth
By going to him of all people on earth
To ask if he knew any fruit to be had
For the picking. The rascal, he said he'd be glad
To tell if he knew. But the year had been bad.
There *had* been some berries – but those were all gone.
He didn't say where they had been. He went on:
"I'm sure – I'm sure" – as polite as could be.
He spoke to his wife in the door, "Let me see,
Mame, *we* don't know any good berrying place?"
It was all he could do to keep a straight face.'

'If he thinks all the fruit that grows wild is for him,
He'll find he's mistaken. See here, for a whim,
We'll pick in the Pattersons' pasture this year.
We'll go in the morning, that is, if it's clear,
And the sun shines out warm: the vines must be wet.
It's so long since I picked I almost forget
How we used to pick berries: we took one look round,
Then sank out of sight like trolls underground,

And saw nothing more of each other, or heard,
Unless when you said I was keeping a bird
Away from its nest, and I said it was you.
"Well, one of us is." For complaining it flew
Around and around us. And then for a while
We picked, till I feared you had wandered a mile,
And I thought I had lost you. I lifted a shout
Too loud for the distance you were, it turned out,
For when you made answer, your voice was as low
As talking – you stood up beside me, you know.'

'We shan't have the place to ourselves to enjoy –
Not likely, when all the young Lorens deploy.
They'll be there tomorrow, or even tonight.
They won't be too friendly – they may be polite –
To people they look on as having no right
To pick where they're picking. But we won't complain.
You ought to have seen how it looked in the rain,
The fruit mixed with water in layers of leaves,
Like two kinds of jewels, a vision for thieves.'

BLUEBERRYING IN AUGUST

Sprung from the hummocks
of this island, stemmed,
sea-spray-fed chromosomes
trait-coded, say, for eyes
of that surprising blue
some have, that you have:
they're everywhere, these
mimic apertures the color
of distances, of drowning –

of creekside bluebells
islanded in the lost world
of childhood; of the
illusory indigo that moats
these hillocks when
the air is windless.

Today, though, there is
wind: a slate sag occludes
the afternoon with old,
hound-throated mutterings.
Offshore, the lighthouse
fades to a sheeted,
sightless ghost. August
grows somber. Though the blue-

eyed chromosome gives way,
living even so, minute to
minute, was never better.

AMY CLAMPITT

BRAMBLEBERRIES, BLACKBERRIES
From the Provençal

Brambleberries, blackberries –
Grown without our pain or powers;
Brambleberries, beggar's gain,
Oh how strongly bring again
Hedgerow searchings, eager hours.

When brown Pomona after heat
Brings lovely and elusive days,
The poor fruit from the past can raise
The taste of childhood, bittersweet.

RUTH PITTER

BLACKBERRYING

Nobody in the lane, and nothing, nothing but
    blackberries,
Blackberries on either side, though on the right mainly,
A blackberry alley, going down in hooks, and a sea
Somewhere at the end of it, heaving. Blackberries
Big as the ball of my thumb, and dumb as eyes
Ebon in the hedges, fat
With blue-red juices. These they squander on my fingers.
I had not asked for such a blood sisterhood; they must
    love me.
They accommodate themselves to my milkbottle,
    flattening their sides.

Overhead go the choughs in black, cacophonous flocks –
Bits of burnt paper wheeling in a blown sky.
Theirs is the only voice, protesting, protesting.
I do not think the sea will appear at all.
The high, green meadows are glowing, as if lit from
    within.
I come to one bush of berries so ripe it is a bush of flies,
Hanging their bluegreen bellies and their wing panes
    in a Chinese screen.
The honey-feast of the berries has stunned them; they
    believe in heaven.
One more hook, and the berries and bushes end.

The only thing to come now is the sea.
From between two hills a sudden wind funnels at me,
Slapping its phantom laundry in my face.
These hills are too green and sweet to have tasted salt.
I follow the sheep path between them. A last hook
     brings me
To the hills' northern face, and the face is orange rock
That looks out on nothing, nothing but a great space
Of white and pewter lights, and a din like silversmiths
Beating and beating at an intractable metal.

TANGERINE EATER

Oh what foresight! This rabbit of the fruit-world. Imagine, in a single specimen thirty-seven small seeds ready to fall just about anywhere and sprout her progeny. We had to fix that. She could have populated the earth – this little determined Mandarin who wears an oversized dress as if she were to grow bigger. In fact, badly dressed: more preoccupied with multiplication than with style. Show her the pomegranate in her armor of Cordova leather: *she* is exploding with future, controls herself, condescends.... And revealing a glimpse of her possible offspring, she suffocates them in a crimson cradle. The earth seems too evasive to enter a pact of abundance with her.

A DISH OF PEACHES IN RUSSIA

With my whole body I taste these peaches,
I touch them and smell them. Who speaks?

I absorb them as the Angevine
Absorbs Anjou. I see them as a lover sees,

As a young lover sees the first buds of spring
And as the black Spaniard plays his guitar.

Who speaks? But it must be that I,
That animal, that Russian, that exile, for whom

The bells of the chapel pullulate sounds at
Heart. The peaches are large and round,

Ah! and red; and they have peach fuzz, ah!
They are full of juice and the skin is soft.

They are full of the colors of my village
And of fair weather, summer, dew, peace.

The room is quiet where they are.
The windows are open. The sunlight fills

The curtains. Even the drifting of the curtains,
Slight as it is, disturbs me. I did not know

That such ferocities could tear
One self from another, as these peaches do.

TROPICAL FRUIT

Oh, stretched amid these orchards of the sun,
Give me to drain the coco's milky bowl,
And from the palm to draw its freshening wine!
More bounteous far than all the frantic juice
Which Bacchus pours. Nor, on its slender twigs
Low-bending, be the full pomegranate scorned;
Nor, creeping through the woods, the gelid race
Of berries. Oft in humble station dwells
Unboastful worth, above fastidious pomp.
Witness, thou best anana, thou the pride
Of vegetable life, beyond whate'er
The poets imaged in the golden age:
Quick let me strip thee of thy tufty coat,
Spread thy ambrosial stores, and feast with Jove!

NINE NECTARINES

Arranged by two's as peaches are,
at intervals that all may live –
eight and a single one, on twigs that
grew the year before – they look like
a derivative;
although not uncommonly
the opposite is seen –
nine peaches on a nectarine.
Fuzzless through slender crescent leaves
of green or blue or
both, in the Chinese style, the four

pairs' half-moon leaf-mosaic turns
out to the sun the sprinkled blush
of puce-American-Beauty pink
applied to beeswax gray by the
uninquiring brush
of mercantile bookbinding.
Like the peach *Yu*, the red-
cheeked peach which cannot aid the dead,
but eaten in time prevents death,
the Italian
peach nut, Persian plum, Ispahan

secluded wall-grown nectarine,
as wild spontaneous fruit was

found in China first. But was it wild?
  Prudent de Candolle would not say.
One perceives no flaws
  in this emblematic group
of nine, with leaf window
unquilted by *curculio*
    which someone once depicted on
      this much-mended plate
      or in the also accurate

    unantlered moose or Iceland horse
or ass asleep against the old
    thick, low-leaning nectarine that is the
    color of the shrub-tree's brownish
flower.

* * *

A Chinese 'understands
the spirit of the wilderness'
    and the nectarine-loving kylin
    of pony appearance – the long-
tailed or the tailless
  small cinnamon-brown, common
camel-haired unicorn
with antelope feet and no horn,
    here enameled on porcelain.
      It was a Chinese
      who imagined this masterpiece.

SUNDAY LEMONS

Desolate lemons, hold
tight, in your bowl of earth,
the light to your bitter flesh,

let a lemon glare
be all your armour
this naked Sunday,

your inflexible light
bounce off the shields of apples
so real they seem waxen,

share your acid silence
with this woman's remembering
Sundays of other fruit,

till by concentration
you grow, a phalanx of helmets
braced for anything,

hexagonal cities where bees
died purely for sweetness,
your lamps be the last to go

on this polished table
this Sunday, which demands
more than the faith of candles

than helmeted conquistadors
dying like bees, multiplying
memories in her golden head;

as the afternoon vagues
into indigo, let your lamps
hold in this darkening earth

bowl, still life, but a life
beyond tears or the gaieties
of dew, the gay, neon damp

of the evening that blurs
the form of this woman lying,
a lemon, a flameless lamp.

A SONG OF BANANAS

Have you no Bananas, simple townsmen all?
    'Nay, but we have them certainly.
'We buy them off the barrows, with the vegetable-
       marrows
    'And the cabbage of our own country,
    '(From the costers of our own country.)'

Those are not Bananas, simple townsmen all.
    (Plantains from Canaryward maybe!)
For the true are red and gold, and they fill no
      steamer's hold,
    But flourish in a rare country,
    (That men go far to see.)

Their stiff fronds point the nooning down, simple
      townsmen all,
    Or rear against the breezes off the sea;
Or duck and loom again, through the curtains of
      the rain
    That the loaded hills let free –
    (Bellying 'twixt the uplands and the sea.)

Little birds inhabit there, simple townsmen all –
    Jewelled things no bigger than a bee;
And the opal butterflies plane and settle, flare and rise,

Through the low-arched greenery,
  (That is malachite and jade of the sea.)

The red earth works and whispers there, simple
      townsmen all,
  Day and night in rank fecundity,
That the Blossom and the Snake lie open and awake,
  As it was by Eden Tree,
  (When the First Moon silvered through the Tree) . . .

But you must go to business, simple townsmen all,
  By 'bus and train and tram and tube must flee!
For your Pharpars and Abanas do not include Bananas
  (And Jordan is a distant stream to drink of, simple
      townsmen),
  Which leaves the more for me!

DAMSON BOY

Yes, they had greens enough,
But fruit – well, he didn't know.
Apart from currants and stuff
Damsons were all they could grow.

Damsons were all they could grow.
Never an apple or plum.
It was cold in those parts, you know;
But he was fond of his home.

Never an apple or pear;
But when damsons were blue
Families gathered there
And shared the dishes they knew.

They had hotpot and damson tart,
Damson jam on a scone,
And made wine that might cheer an old heart
Long after the children were gone.

Dancing black eyes he had;
Spoke kindly, though he was shy.
Smallish neat-featured lad,
A credit to damson pie.

RUTH PITTER

AUTUMN FRUITS

Obedient to the breeze and beating ray,
From the deep-loaded bough a mellow shower
Incessant melts away. The juicy pear
Lies in a soft profusion scattered round.
A various sweetness swells the gentle race,
By Nature's all-refining hand prepared,
Of tempered sun, and water, earth, and air,
In ever-changing composition mixed.
Such, falling frequent through the chiller night,
The fragrant stores, the wide-projected heaps
Of apples, which the lusty-handed year
Innumerous o'er the blushing orchard shakes.
A various spirit, fresh, delicious, keen,
Dwells in their gelid pores, and active points
The piercing cider for the thirsty tongue –
Thy native theme, and boon inspirer too,
Phillips, Pomona's bard! the second thou
Who nobly durst in rhyme-unfettered verse
With British freedom sing the British song –
How from Silurian vats high-sparkling wines
Foam in transparent floods, some strong to cheer
The wintry revels of the labouring hind,
And tasteful some to cool the summer hours.

From A KUMQUAT FOR JOHN KEATS

Today I found the right fruit for my prime,
not orange, not tangelo, and not lime,
nor moon-like globes of grapefruit that now hang
outside our bedroom, nor tart lemon's tang
(though last year full of bile and self-defeat
I wanted to believe no life was sweet)
nor the tangible sunshine of the tangerine,
and no incongruous citrus ever seen
at greengrocers' in Newcastle or Leeds
mis-spelt by the spuds and mud-caked swedes,
a fruit an older poet might substitute
for the grape John Keats thought fit to be Joy's fruit,
when, two years before he died, he tried to write
how Melancholy dwelled inside Delight,
and if he'd known the citrus that I mean
that's not orange, lemon, lime or tangerine,
I'm pretty sure that Keats, though he had heard
'of candied apple, quince and plum and gourd'
instead of 'grape against the palate fine'
would have, if he'd known it, plumped for mine,
this Eastern citrus scarcely cherry size
he'd bite just once and then apostrophize
and pen one stanza how the fruit had all
the qualities of fruit before the Fall,
but in the next few lines be forced to write

how Eve's apple tasted at the second bite,
and if John Keats had only lived to be,
because of extra years, in need like me,
at 42 he'd help me celebrate
that Micanopy kumquat that I ate
whole, straight off the tree, sweet pulp and sour skin –
or was it sweet outside, and sour within?
For however many kumquats that I eat
I'm not sure if it's flesh or rind that's sweet,
and being a man of doubt at life's mid-way
I'd offer Keats some kumquats and I'd say:
You'll find that one part's sweet and one part's tart:
say where the sweetness or the sourness start.

VEGETABLES

LAST YEAR'S PICNIC

Here it's rose-time again, chick-peas in season,
cabbages, Sosylus, first heads of the year,
fillets of smelt, fresh-salted cheese,
tender and furled up lettuce leaves . . .
but we don't go way out to the point, Sosylus,
or picnic, as we used to, on the overlook.
Antigenes and Bacchios had the old party spirit,
but today we dump them in their graves.

EPIGRAM XI.31

Gourds get a raw deal with Caecilius,
Cut, sliced and diced in little pieces – thus
Atreus made his nephews into martyrs.
You dine with him – he'll give you gourds for starters,
Gourds for the first, likewise the second course,
Then comes the third, and they turn up in force.
Even for dessert you cannot well escape,
The gourds come in confectionery shape –
A baker's feeble effort – dates as well,
Like those small gilded ones the theatres sell;
Then strange concoctions from behind the scenes,
Fine imitation mincemeats, lentils, beans,
Tunny's tail, salt-fish, will appear to greet us,
Black-pudding and the edible boletus.
The storekeeper has tried experiments
With leaves of rue and various flavouring scents
And made Capellian sweetmeats. Choice and rare
All looks, displayed in stylish manner there
On tiny saucer or great shining plate –
A lovely feast, laid out in splendid state;
But to the host – a lovelier thought than any –
To lay all this on, he's laid out one penny.

ROSEMARY

Beauty and Beauty's son and rosemary –
Venus and Love, her son, to speak plainly –
born of the sea supposedly,
at Christmas each, in company,
braids a garland of festivity.
  Not always rosemary –

since the flight to Egypt, blooming differently.
With lancelike leaf, green but silver underneath,
its flowers – white originally –
turned blue. The herb of memory,
imitating the blue robe of Mary,
  is not too legendary

to flower both as symbol and as pungency.
Springing from stones beside the sea,
the height of Christ when thirty-three,
it feeds on dew and to the bee
'hath a dumb language'; is in reality
  a kind of Christmas tree.

MARIANNE MOORE   99

EATING BAMBOO-SHOOTS

My new Province is a land of bamboo-groves:
Their shoots in spring fill the valleys and hills.
The mountain woodman cuts an armful of them
And brings them down to sell at the early market.
Things are cheap in proportion as they are common;
For two farthings I buy a whole bundle.
I put the shoots in a great earthen pot
And heat them up along with boiling rice.
The purple skins broken – like an old brocade;
The white skin opened – like new pearls.
Now every day I eat them recklessly;
For a long time I have not touched meat.
All the time I was living at Lo-yang
They could not give me enough to suit my taste.
Now I can have as many shoots as I please;
For each breath of the south-wind makes a
        new bamboo!

        TRANS. ARTHUR WALEY

YAM

Rind and resurrection, hell and seed,
Fire-folia, hotbeds of a casserole
Divinely humble, it awaits your need.
Its message, taken in by you,

Deep reds obliterate. Be glad they do.
Go now by upward stages, fortified,
Where an imaginary line is being
Drawn past which you do not melt, you suffer

Pure form's utter discontent, white waste
And wintry grazing, flocks of white
But with no shepherd-sage, no flute, no phrases;
Parchment frozen, howling pricksong, mute

Periods that flash and stun –
Hit on the head, who brought you to this pass?
Valleys far below are spouting
Baby slogans and green gripes of spring,

Clogged pools, the floating yen . . .
You feel someone take leave, at once
Transfiguring, transfigured. A voice grunts
MATTER YOU MERELY DO I AM

Which lies on snow in dark ideogram
– Or as a later commentary words it,
One-night's-meat-another-morning's-mass-
Against-inhuman-odds-I-celebrate.

JAMES MERRILL

PEAS

I always eat peas with honey,
I've done it all my life,
They do taste kind of funny,
But it keeps them on the knife.

THE BROAD BEAN SERMON

Beanstalks, in any breeze, are a slack church parade
without belief, saying *trespass against us* in unison,
recruits in mint Air Force dacron, with unbuttoned
    leaves.

Upright with water like men, square in stem-section
they grow to great lengths, drink rain, keel over all ways,
kink down and grow up afresh, with proffered new
    greenstuff.

Above the cat-and-mouse floor of a thin bean forest
snails hang rapt in their food, ants hurry through
    several dimensions:
spiders tense and sag like little black flags in their
    cordage.

Going out to pick beans with the sun high as fence-
    tops, you find
plenty, and fetch them. An hour or a cloud later
you find shirtfulls more. At every hour of daylight

appear more than you missed: ripe, knobbly ones,
    fleshy-sided,
thin-straight, thin-crescent, frown-shaped, bird-
    shouldered, boat-keeled ones,

103

beans knuckled and single-bulged, minute green
>dolphins at suck,

beans upright like lecturing, outstretched like blessing
>fingers
in the incident light, and more still, oblique to your
>notice
that the noon glare or cloud-light or afternoon slants
>will uncover

till you ask yourself Could I have overlooked so many, or
do they form in an hour? unfolding into reality
like templates for subtly broad grins, like unique caught
>expressions,

like edible meanings, each sealed around with a string
and affixed to its moment, an unceasing colloquial
>assembly,
the portly, the stiff, and those lolling in pointed green
>slippers . . .

Wondering who'll take the spare bagfulls, you grin with
>happiness
— it is your health — you vow to pick them all
even the last few, weeks off yet, misshapen as toes.

MUSHROOMS

Overnight, very
Whitely, discreetly,
Very quietly

Our toes, our noses
Take hold on the loam,
Acquire the air.

Nobody sees us,
Stops us, betrays us;
The small grains make room.

Soft fists insist on
Heaving the needles,
The leafy bedding,

Even the paving.
Our hammers, our rams,
Earless and eyeless,

Perfectly voiceless,
Widen the crannies,
Shoulder through holes. We

Diet on water,
On crumbs of shadow,
Bland-mannered, asking

Little or nothing.
So many of us!
So many of us!

We are shelves, we are
Tables, we are meek,
We are edible,

Nudgers and shovers
In spite of ourselves.
Our kind multiplies:

We shall by morning
Inherit the earth.
Our foot's in the door.

SWEDES

They have taken the gable from the roof of clay
On the long swede pile. They have let in the sun
To the white and gold and purple of curled fronds
Unsunned. It is a sight more tender-gorgeous
At the wood-corner where Winter moans and drips
Than when, in the Valley of the Tombs of Kings,
A boy crawls down into a Pharaoh's tomb
And, first of Christian men, beholds the mummy,
God and monkey, chariot and throne and vase,
Blue pottery, alabaster, and gold.

But dreamless long-dead Amen-hotep lies.
This is a dream of Winter, sweet as Spring.

THE MANGEL-BURY

It was after war; Edward Thomas had fallen at Arras –
I was walking by Gloucester musing on such things
As fill his verse with goodness; it was February;
    the long house
Straw-thatched of the mangels stretched two wide
    wings;
And looked as part of the earth heaped up by
    dead soldiers
In the most fitting place – along the hedge's yet-bare
    lines.
West spring breathed there early, that none foreign
    divines.
Across the flat country the rattling of the cart sounded;
Heavy of wood, jingling of iron; as he neared me
    I waited
For the chance perhaps of heaving at those great
    rounded
Ruddy or orange things – and right to be rolled
    and hefted
By a body like mine, soldier still, and clean from water.
Silent he assented; till the cart was drifted
High with those creatures, so right in size and matter.
We threw with our bodies swinging, blood in my ears
    singing;
His was the thick-set sort of farmer, but well-built –

Perhaps, long before, his blood's name ruled all,
Watched all things for his own. If my luck had so
        willed
Many questions of lordship I had heard him tell – old
Names, rumours. But my pain to more moving called
And him to some barn business far in the fifteen acre
        field.

POTATO
For André du Bouchet

An underground grower, blind and a common brown;
Got a misshapen look, it's nudged where it could;
Simple as soil yet crowded as earth with all.

Cut open raw, it looses a cool clean stench,
Mineral acid seeping from pores of prest meal;
It is like breaching a strangely refreshing tomb:

Therein the taste of first stones, the hands of dead slaves,
Waters men drank in the earliest frightful woods,
Flint chips, and peat, and the cinders of buried camps.

Scrubbed under faucet water the planet skin
Polishes yellow, but tears to the plain insides;
Parching, the white's blue-hearted like hungry hands.

All of the cold dark kitchens, and war-frozen gray
Evening at window; I remember so many
Peeling potatoes quietly into chipt pails.

'It was potatoes saved us, they kept us alive.'
Then they had something to say akin to praise
For the mean earth-apples, too common to cherish
     or steal.

110

Times being hard, the Sikh and the Senegalese,
Hobo and Okie, the body of Jesus the Jew,
Vestigial virtues, are eaten; we shall survive.

What has not lost its savor shall hold us up,
And we are praising what saves us, what fills the need.
(Soon there'll be packets again, with Algerian fruits.)

Oh, it will not bear polish, the ancient potato,
Needn't be nourished by Caesars, will blow anywhere,
Hidden by nature, counted-on, stubborn and blind.

You may have noticed the bush that it pushes to air,
Comical-delicate, sometimes with second-rate flowers
Awkward and milky and beautiful only to hunger.

RICHARD WILBUR   111

RECIPE FOR A SALAD

To make this condiment, your poet begs
The pounded yellow of two hard-boiled eggs;
Two boiled potatoes, passed through kitchen-sieve,
Smoothness and softness to the salad give;
Let onion atoms lurk within the bowl,
And, half-suspected, animate the whole.
Of mordant mustard add a single spoon,
Distrust the condiment that bites so soon;
But deem it not, thou man of herbs, a fault,
To add a double quantity of salt.
And, lastly, o'er the flavored compound toss
A magic soup-spoon of anchovy sauce.
Oh, green and glorious! Oh, herbaceous treat!
'T would tempt the dying anchorite to eat,
Back to the world he'd turn his fleeting soul,
And plunge his fingers in the salad bowl!
Serenely full, the epicure would say,
Fate can not harm me, I have dined to-day!

SALAD

There, at no cost, on onions, rank and red,
Or the curl'd endive's bitter leaf, he fed:
On scallions sliced, or with a sensual gust
On rockets – foul provocatives of lust;
Nor even shunn'd, with smarting gums, to press
Nasturtium, pungent face-distorting mess!
Some such regale now also in his thought,
With hasty steps his garden-ground he sought;
There delving with his hands, he first displaced
Four plants of garlick, large, and rooted fast;
The tender tops of parsley next he culls,
Then the old rue-bush shudders as he pulls,
And coriander last to these succeeds,
That hangs on slightest threads her trembling seeds.
Placed near his sprightly fire he now demands
The mortar at his sable servant's hands;
When stripping all his garlick first, he tore
The exterior coats, and cast them on the floor,
Then cast away with like contempt the skin,
Flimsier concealment of the cloves within.
These search'd, and perfect found, he one by one
Rinsed, and disposed within the hollow stone;
Salt added, and a lump of salted cheese,
With his injected herbs he cover'd these,
And tucking with his left his tunic tight,

And seizing fast the pestle with his right,
The garlick bruising first he soon express'd,
And mix'd the various juices of the rest.
He grinds, and by degrees his herbs below
Lost in each other their own powers forego
And with the cheese in compound, to the sight
Nor wholly green appear, nor wholly white.
His nostrils oft the forceful fume resent;
He cursed full oft his dinner for its scent,
Or with wry faces, wiping as he spoke
The trickling tears, cried – 'Vengeance on the smoke!'
The work proceeds: not roughly turns he now
The pestle, but in circles smooth and slow;
With cautious hand that grudges what it spills,
Some drops of olive-oil he next instils;
Then vinegar with caution scarcely less;
And gathering to a ball the medley mess,
Last, with two fingers frugally applied,
Sweeps the small remnant from the mortar's side:
And thus complete in figure and in kind,
Obtains at length the Salad he design'd.

BROW

O cool in the summer is salad,
 And warm in the winter is love;
And a poet shall sing you a ballad
 Delicious thereon and thereof.
A singer am I, if no sinner,
 My Muse has a marvellous wing,
And I willingly worship at dinner
 The Sirens of Spring.

Take endive ... like love it is bitter;
 Take beet ... for like love it is red;
Crisp leaf of the lettuce shall glitter,
 And cress from the rivulet's bed;
Anchovies foam-born, like the Lady
 Whose beauty has maddened this bard;
And olives, from groves that are shady;
 And eggs – boil 'em hard.

MORTIMER COLLINS,   115
AFTER ALGERNON SWINBURNE

DELICATESSEN

IN SCHRAFFT'S

Having finished the Blue-plate Special
And reached the coffee stage,
Stirring her cup she sat,
A somewhat shapeless figure
Of indeterminate age
In an undistinguished hat.

When she lifted her eyes it was plain
That our globular furore,
Our international rout
Of sin and apparatus
And dying men galore,
Was not being bothered about.

Which of the seven heavens
Was responsible her smile
Wouldn't be sure but attested
That, whoever it was, a god
Worth kneeling-to for a while
Had tabernacled and rested.

GOOSEBERRY FOOL

The gooseberry's no doubt an oddity,
an outlaw or pariah even – thorny
and tart as any
kindergarten martinet, it can harbor
like a fernseed, on its leaves' under-
side, bad news for pine trees,
whereas the spruce
resists the blister rust
it's host to. That veiny Chinese
lantern, its stolid jelly
of a fruit, not only has
no aroma but is twice as tedious
as the wild strawberry's sunburst
stem-end appendage: each one must
be between-nail-snipped at both extremities.

Altogether, gooseberry virtues
take some getting
used to, much as does trepang,
tripe à la mode de Caen,
or having turned thirteen.
The acerbity of all things green
and adolescent lingers in
it – the arrogant, shrinking,
prickling-in-every-direction thorn-
iness that loves no company except its,

or anyhow that's what it gets:
bristling up through gooseberry ghetto sprawl
are braced thistles' silvery, militantly symmetrical
defense machineries. Likewise inseparably en-
tangled in the disarray of an
uncultivated childhood, where gooseberry bushes (since
rooted out) once flourished, is
the squandered volupté of lemon-
yellow-petaled roses' luscious flimflam –
an inkling of the mingling into one experience
of suave and sharp, whose supremely im-
probable and far-fetched culinary
embodiment is a gooseberry fool.

Tomorrow, having stumbled into
this trove of chief ingredients
(the other being very thickest cream)
I'll demonstrate it for you. Ever since,
four summers ago, I brought you,
a gleeful Ariel, the trophy
of a small sour handful,
I've wondered what not quite articulated thing
could render magical
the green globe of an unripe berry.
I think now it was simply
the great globe itself's too much to carry.

AMY CLAMPITT   121

HONEY

Beeman Cliton hews
From the flower-fed hive
Sweet honey-crop, Spring's
Gift, ambrosial, pressed
From combs of his far-
Roving flock ... Let but his
Multitude of singing bees
Fill full with honeyed wine
Their wax-built cells.

APOLLONIDES
TRANS. PETER WHIGHAM

THE HONEYCOMB

If thou hast found an honeycomb,
Eat thou not all, but taste on some:
For if thou eat'st it to excess,
That sweetness turns to loathsomeness.
Taste it to temper, then 'twill be
Marrow and manna unto thee.

HIGH SUGAR

Honey gave sweetness
to Athens and Rome,
and later, when splendour
might rise nearer home,

sweetness was still honey
since, pious or lax,
every cloister had its apiary
for honey and wax

but when kings and new doctrines
drained those deep hives
then millions of people
were shipped from their lives

to grow the high sugar
from which were refined
frigates, perukes, human races
and the liberal mind.

CHOCOLATES

Once some people were visiting Chekhov.
While they made remarks about his genius
the Master fidgeted. Finally
he said, 'Do you like chocolates?'

They were astonished, and silent.
He repeated the question,
whereupon one lady plucked up her courage
and murmured shyly, 'Yes.'

'Tell me,' he said, leaning forward,
light glinting from his spectacles,
'what kind? The light, sweet chocolate
or the dark, bitter kind?'

The conversation became general.
They spoke of cherry centers,
of almonds and Brazil nuts.
Losing their inhibitions
they interrupted one another.
For people may not know what they think
about politics in the Balkans,
or the vexed question of men and women,
but everyone has a definite opinion
about the flavor of shredded coconut.

Finally someone spoke of chocolates filled with liqueur,
and everyone, even the author of *Uncle Vanya*,
was at a loss for words.

As they were leaving he stood by the door
and took their hands.
                    In the coach returning to Petersburg
they agreed that it had been a most
unusual conversation.

ICE CREAM

'Ice cream!' Sun. Light airy cakes.
A clear glass tumbler of water, icy cold.
Our dreams take flight, into a chocolate world
Of rosy dawns on milky Alpine peaks.

But as the teaspoon tinkles, it is sweet
In some little summerhouse amid the dry acacias,
To gaze, then take gratefully from tearoom Graces,
Little whorled cups with crumbly things to eat...

The street-organ's playmate suddenly appears,
The ice-cream cart, with multicolored covering –
The chest is full of lovely frozen things;
With greedy attentiveness, a small boy peers.

And what will he choose? The gods themselves
    can't say:
A diamond tart? A wafer filled with cream?
But under his slender spoon the divine ice,
Glittering in the sun, will soon melt away.

A GRACE FOR ICE-CREAM

For water-ices, cheap but good,
That find us in a thirsty mood;
For ices made of milk or cream
That slip down smoothly as a dream;
For cornets, sandwiches and pies
That make the gastric juices rise;
For ices bought in little shops
Or at the kerb from him who stops;
For chanting of the sweet refrain:
'Vanilla, strawberry or plain?'
    We thank Thee, Lord, who sendst with heat
    This cool deliciousness to eat.

ALLAN M. LAING

From EPISTLE TO MRS TYLER

First then for custards, my dear Mary,
The produce of your dainty dairy.
For stew'd, for bak'd, for boil'd, for roast,
And all the teas and all the toast;
With thankful tongue and bowing attitude,
I here present you with my gratitude:
Next for your apples, pears and plumbs
Acknowledgment in order comes;
For wine, for ale, for fowl, for fish – for
Ev'n all one's appetite can wish for:
But O ye pens, and O ye pencils,
And all ye scribbling utensils,
Say in what words and in what metre,
Shall unfeign'd admiration greet her,
For that rich banquet so refin'd
Her conversation gave the mind;
The solid meal of sense and worth,
Set off by the desert of mirth;
Wit's fruit and pleasure's genial bowl,
And all the joyous flow of soul;
For these, and every kind ingredient
That form'd your love – your most obedient.

WRITTEN ON A PAPER WHICH CONTAINED A PIECE OF BRIDE CAKE GIVEN TO THE AUTHOR BY A LADY

Ye curious hands, that, hid from vulgar eyes,
By search profane shall find this hallowed cake,
With virtue's awe forbear the sacred prize,
Nor dare a theft for love and pity's sake!

This precious relic, formed by magic power,
Beneath her shepherd's haunted pillow laid,
Was meant by love to charm the silent hour,
The secret present of a matchless maid.

The Cyprian queen, at Hymen's fond request,
Each nice ingredient chose with happiest art;
Fears, sighs and wishes of the enamoured breast,
And pains that please, are mixed in every part.

With rosy hand the spicy fruit she brought,
From Paphian hills and fair Cythera's isle;
And tempered sweet with these the melting thought,
The kiss ambrosial and the yielding smile;

Ambiguous looks, that scorn and yet relent,
Denials mild and firm unaltered truth,
Reluctant pride and amorous faint consent,
And meeting ardours and exulting youth.

Sleep, wayward god! hath sworn, while these remain,
With flattering dreams to dry his nightly tear,
And cheerful Hope, so oft invoked in vain,
With fairy songs shall soothe his pensive ear.

If, bound by vows to friendship's gentle side,
And fond of soul, thou hop'st an equal grace,
If youth or maid thy joys and griefs divide,
O much intreated, leave this fatal place.

Sweet Peace, who long hath shunned my plaintive day,
Consents at length to bring me short delight:
Thy careless steps may scare her doves away,
And grief with raven note usurp the night.

THE BUN

The muffin and the crumpet are
    When adequately done
A dish to make a curate wish
    To excel in feats of fun;
A Canon booms, 'tis said, when fed
    On toasted Sallie Lunn;
E'en Deans, I ween, plum cake being seen,
    Have been observed to run:
But, Ah! a Bishop come to tea!
    He takes the Bun.

A PIECE OF CAKE

This New York baker's bread's described as 'Swiss'
though it's said there's something Nazi in their past.
But the cheesecake that they make 's the best there is.
It's made fresh every day and sells out fast.

My kids are coming so I buy one too,
and ask for a WELCOME frosted on the top.
I watch the tube squeeze out the script in blue.
It has my father's smell, this German's shop,
as he concentrates on his ice craftsmanship
that cost him weeks of evenings to complete,
a cake with V signs, spitfires, landing strip,
that took too many pains to cut and eat
to welcome home a niece back from the WAAFs.

Already I feel the cake stick in my throat!

The icing tube flows freely and then coughs.

The frosting comes out Gothic and reads: 𝕿𝕺𝕯!

OFFERING

A yellow-coated pomegranate, figs like lizards' necks,
    a handful of half-rosy part-ripe grapes,
a quince all delicate-downed and fragrant-fleeced,
    a walnut winking out from its green shell,
a cucumber with the bloom on it pouting from its leaf-bed,
    and a ripe gold-coated olive – dedicated
to Priapus friend of travellers, by Lamon the gardener,
    begging strength for his limbs and his trees.

From THE ALCHEMIST

We will be brave, Puffe, now we have the med'cine
My meat shall all come in, in Indian shells,
Dishes of agate, set in gold, and studded
With emeralds, sapphires, hyacinths, and rubies,
The tongues of carps, dormice, and camels' heels,
Boil'd in the spirit of sol, *and dissolv'd pearl,*
Apicius' diet 'gainst the epilepsy:
And I will eat these broths with spoon of amber,
Headed with diamond and carbuncle.
My foot-boy shall eat pheasants, calver'd salmons,
Knots, godwits, lampreys: I myself will have
The beards of barbels serv'd, instead of salads;
Oil'd mushrooms; and the swelling, unctuous paps
Of a fat pregnant sow, newly cut off,
Drest with an exquisite and poignant sauce,
For which I'll say unto my cook, 'There's gold;
Go forth, and be a knight.'

From THE BATTLE OF THE SUMMER ISLANDS (CANTO 1)

> *What fruits they have, and how Heaven smiles*
> *Upon those late-discovered isles.*

Aid me, Bellona! while the dreadful fight
Betwixt a nation and two whales I write.
Seas stained with gore I sing, adventurous toil,
And how these monsters did disarm an isle.
   Bermudas, walled with rocks, who does not know?
That happy island where huge lemons grow,
And orange trees, which golden fruit do bear,
The Hesperian garden boasts of none so fair;
Where shining pearl, coral, and many a pound,
On the rich shore, of ambergris is found.
The lofty cedar, which to heaven aspires,
The prince of trees! is fuel for their fires;
The smoke by which their loaded spits do turn,
For incense might on sacred altars burn;
Their private roofs on odorous timber borne,
Such as might palaces for kings adorn.
The sweet palmettos a new Bacchus yield,
With leaves as ample as the broadest shield,
Under the shadow of whose friendly boughs
They sit, carousing where their liquor grows.
Figs there unplanted through the fields do grow,
Such as fierce Cato did the Romans show,

With the rare fruit inviting them to spoil
Carthage, the mistress of so rich a soil.
The naked rocks are not unfruitful there,
But, at some constant seasons, every year,
Their barren tops with luscious food abound,
And with the eggs of various fowls are crowned.
Tobacco is the worst of things, which they
To English landlords, as their tribute, pay.
Such is the mould, that the blessed tenant feeds
On precious fruits, and pays his rent in weeds.
With candied plantains, and the juicy pine,
On choicest melons, and sweet grapes, they dine,
And with potatoes fat their wanton swine.
Nature these cates with such a lavish hand
Pours out among them, that our coarser land
Tastes of that bounty, and does cloth return,
Which not for warmth, but ornament, is worn;
For the kind spring, which but salutes us here,
Inhabits there, and courts them all the year.
Ripe fruits and blossoms on the same trees live;
At once they promise what at once they give.
So sweet the air, so moderate the clime,
None sickly lives, or dies before his time.
Heaven sure has kept this spot of earth uncursed
To show how all things were created first.
The tardy plants in our cold orchards placed,
Reserve their fruit for the next age's taste.

There a small grain in some few months will be
A firm, a lofty, and a spacious tree.
The palma-christi, and the fair papà,
Now but a seed, (preventing nature's law)
In half the circle of the hasty year
Project a shade, and lovely fruit do wear.
And as their trees, in our dull region set,
But faintly grow, and no perfection get;
So, in this northern tract, our hoarser throats,
Utter unripe and ill-constrainèd notes,
Where the supporter of the poets' style,
Phœbus, on them eternally does smile.
Oh! how I long my careless limbs to lay
Under the plantain's shade, and all the day
With amorous airs my fancy entertain,
Invoke the Muses, and improve my vein!
No passion there in my free breast should move,
None but the sweet and best of passions, love.
There while I sing, if gentle love be by,
That tunes my lute, and winds the strings so high,
With the sweet sound of Sacharissa's name
I'll make the listening savages grow tame. –
But while I do these pleasing dreams indite,
I am diverted from the promised fight.

EDMUND WALLER   137

A SIMPLE FEAST

Here are grapes ready to turn to wine,
pieces of pomegranate ready split,
yellow marrow of seashore escargots,
almonds terrible to bite on, bees'
ambrosia, short-cake with sesame,
sweet cloves of garlic, pears with glassy pips,
ample interludes for the drinker's stomach:
for Pan with his crook, Priapus with his horn,
this simple feast, from Philoxenides.

THE POET, THE OYSTER, AND
THE SENSITIVE PLANT

An Oyster cast upon the shore
Was heard, though never heard before,
Complaining in a speech well worded,
And worthy thus to be recorded:
　　Ah hapless wretch! condemn'd to dwell
For ever in my native shell,
Ordain'd to move when others please,
Not for my own content or ease,
But toss'd and buffeted about,
Now *in* the water, and now *out*.
'Twere better to be born a stone
Of ruder shape and feeling none,
Than with a tenderness like mine,
And sensibilities so fine!
I envy that unfeeling shrub,
Fast-rooted against every rub.
The plant he meant grew not far off,
And felt the sneer with scorn enough,
Was hurt, disgusted, mortified,
And with asperity replied.
　　When, cry the botanists, and stare,
Did plants call'd Sensitive grow there?
No matter when – a poet's muse is
To make them grow just where she chooses.

139

You shapeless nothing in a dish,
You that are but almost a fish,
I scorn your coarse insinuation,
And have most plentiful occasion
To wish myself the rock I view,
Or such another dolt as you.
For many a grave and learned clerk,
And many a gay unletter'd spark,
With curious touch examines me,
If I can feel as well as he;
And when I bend, retire, and shrink,
Says, well — 'tis more than one would think. —
Thus life is spent, oh fie upon't!
In being touch'd, and crying, don't.

    A poet in his evening walk,
O'erheard and check'd this idle talk.
And your fine sense, he said, and yours,
Whatever evil it endures,
Deserves not, if so soon offended,
Much to be pitied or commended.
Disputes though short, are far too long,
Where both alike are in the wrong;
Your feelings in their full amount,
Are all upon your own account.

    You in your grotto-work enclosed
Complain of being thus exposed,
Yet nothing feel in that rough coat,

Save when the knife is at your throat,
Wherever driven by wind or tide,
Exempt from every ill beside.
    And as for you, my Lady Squeamish,
Who reckon every touch a blemish,
If all the plants that can be found
Embellishing the scene around,
Should droop and wither where they grow,
You would not feel at all, not you.
The noblest minds their virtue prove
By pity, sympathy, and love;
These, these are feelings truly fine,
And prove their owner half divine.
    His censure reach'd them as he dealt it,
And each by shrinking show'd he felt it.

ODE ON A JAR OF PICKLES

A sweet, acidulous, down-reaching thrill
    Pervades my sense: I seem to see or hear
The lushy garden-grounds of Greenwich Hill
    In autumn, when the crispy leaves are sere:
And odours haunt me of remotest spice
    From the Levant or musky-aired Cathay,
Or from the saffron-fields of Jericho,
           Where everything is nice:
    The more I sniff, the more I swoon away,
And what else mortal palate craves, forgo.

Odours unsmelled are keen, but those I smell
    Are keener; wherefore let me sniff again!
Enticing walnuts, I have known ye well
    In youth, when pickles were a passing pain;
Unwitting youth, that craves the candy stem,
    And sugar-plums to olives doth prefer,
And even licks the pots of marmalade
           When sweetness clings to them:
    But now I dream of ambergris and myrrh,
Tasting these walnuts in the poplar shade.

Lo! hoarded coolness in the heart of noon,
    Plucked with its dew, the cucumber is here,
As to the Dryad's parching lips a boon,

And crescent bean-pods, unto Bacchus dear;
And, last of all, the pepper's pungent globe,
　　The scarlet dwelling of the sylph of fire,
Provoking purple draughts; and, surfeited,
　　　　　　I cast my trailing robe
　　O'er my pale feet, touch up my tuneless lyre,
And twist the Delphic wreath to suit my head.

Here shall my tongue in other wise be soured
　　Than fretful men's in parched and palsied days;
And, by the mid-May's dusky leaves embowered,
　　Forget the fruitful blame, the scanty praise.
No sweets to them who sweet themselves were born,
　　Whose natures ooze with lucent saccharine;
Who, with sad repetition soothly cloyed,
　　　　　　The lemon-tinted morn
　　Enjoy, and find acetic twilight fine:
Wake I, or sleep? The pickle-jar is void.

EPIGRAM V.78

Toranius, if the prospect of a cheerless, solitary dinner
Bores you, eat with me – and get thinner.
If you like appetite-whetters,
There'll be cheap Cappadocian lettuce,
Pungent leeks, and tunny-fish
Nestling in sliced eggs. Next, a black earthenware dish
(Watch out – a finger-scorcher!) of broccoli just taken
From its cool bed, pale beans with pink bacon,
And a sausage sitting in the centre
Of a snow-white pudding of polenta.
If you want to try a dessert, I can offer you raisins
    (my own),
Pears (from Syria), and hot chestnuts (grown
In Naples, city of learning)
Roasted in a slow-burning
Fire. As for the wine, by drinking it you'll commend it.
When this great feast has ended,
If, as he well might,
Bacchus stirs up a second appetite,
You'll be reinforced by choice Picenian olives fresh
    from the trees,
Warm lupins and hot chick-peas.
Let's face it,
It's a poor sort of dinner; yet, if you deign to grace it,
You'll neither say nor hear

One word that's not sincere,
You can lounge at ease in your place,
Wearing your own face,
You won't have to listen while your host reads aloud
     from some thick book
Or be forced to look
At girls from that sink, Cadiz, prancing
Through the interminable writhings of professional
     belly-dancing.
Instead, Condylus, my little slave,
Will pipe to us – something not too rustic, nor yet
     too grave.
Well, that's the 'banquet'. I shall invite
Claudia to sit on my left. Who would you like on
     my right?

MARTIAL   145
TRANS. JAMES MICHIE

THE FOOD OF LOVE

I AM A PEACH TREE

I am a peach tree blossoming in a deep pit.
Who is there I may turn to and smile?
You are the moon up in the far sky;
Passing, you looked down on me an hour; then went
     on forever.

A sword with the keenest edge,
Could not cut the stream of water in twain
So that it would cease to flow.
My thought is like the stream; and flows and follows
     you on forever.

TRANS. SHIGEYOSHI OBATA

WILD PEACHES

When the world turns completely upside down
You say we'll emigrate to the Eastern Shore
Aboard a river-boat from Baltimore;
We'll live among wild peach trees, miles from town,
You'll wear a coonskin cap, and I a gown
Homespun, dyed butternut's dark gold colour.
Lost, like your lotus-eating ancestor,
We'll swim in milk and honey till we drown.

The winter will be short, the summer long,
The autumn amber-hued, sunny and hot,
Tasting of cider and of scuppernong;
All seasons sweet, but autumn best of all.
The squirrels in their silver fur will fall
Like falling leaves, like fruit, before your shot.

*　　*　　*

The autumn frosts will lie upon the grass
Like bloom on grapes of purple-brown and gold.
The misted early mornings will be cold;
The little puddles will be roofed with glass.
The sun, which burns from copper into brass,
Melts these at noon, and makes the boys unfold
Their knitted mufflers; full as they can hold,
Fat pockets dribble chestnuts as they pass.

Peaches grow wild, and pigs can live in clover;
A barrel of salted herrings lasts a year;
The spring begins before the winter's over.
By February you may find the skins
Of garter snakes and water moccasins
Dwindled and harsh, dead-white and cloudy-clear.

ELINOR WYLIE

CHERRY

She said, 'Now give me flesh to eat,
flesh of the cherry, dark and sweet.
Bring me a singing bird – the pale
moonlight, the attending nightingale.'

'A languishing poet, too?' I said,
kneeling beside our tumbled bed,
'a poet wan, whose young desire
renews just verses with its fire?'

'Bad dearest, must you tease and tease?
Leave him to rhyming, if you please.'
She smiled. 'Come, give me flesh to eat,
flesh of the cherry, dark and sweet.'

THE ORANGE

At lunchtime I bought a huge orange –
The size of it made us all laugh.
I peeled it and shared it with Robert and Dave –
They got quarters and I had a half.

And that orange, it made me so happy,
As ordinary things often do
Just lately. The shopping. A walk in the park.
This is peace and contentment. It's new.

The rest of the day was quite easy.
I did all the jobs on my list
And enjoyed them and had some time over.
I love you. I'm glad I exist.

WENDY COPE   153

THE ORANGES

The oranges of the Island are like blazing fire
Amongst the emerald boughs
And the lemons are like the paleness of a lover
Who has spent the night crying . . .

ABD UR-RAHMAN IBN MOHAMMED IBN OMAR
TRANS. ANON.

POMEGRANATE

A pomegranate just splitting, a peach just furry,
a fig with wrinkled flesh and juicy bottom,
a purple cluster (thick-berried well of wine),
nuts just skinned from their green peelings – these
the guardian of the fruit lays here for Priapus:
for this single shaft in the wilds, the seed of trees.

154   DIODOROS ZONAS
        TRANS. ALISTAIR ELLIOT

FIGS

The proper way to eat a fig, in society,
Is to split it in four, holding it by the stump,
And open it, so that it is a glittering, rosy, moist,
    honied, heavy-petalled four-petalled flower.

Then you throw away the skin
Which is just like a four-petalled calyx,
After you have taken off the blossom with your lips.

But the vulgar way
Is just to put your mouth to the crack and take out the
    flesh in one bite.

Every fruit has its secret.
The fig is a very secretive fruit.
As you see it standing growing, you feel at once it is
    symbolic:
And it seems male.
But when you come to know it better, you agree with
    the Romans, it is female.

The Italians vulgarly say, it stands for the female part;
    the fig-fruit:
The fissure, the yoni,
The wonderful moist conductivity towards the centre.

Involved,
Inturned,
The flowering all inward and womb-fibrilled;
And but one orifice.

The fig, the horse-shoe, the squash-blossom.
Symbols.

There was a flower that flowered inward, womb-ward;
Now there is a fruit like a ripe womb.
It was always a secret.
That's how it should be, the female should always
    be secret.

There never was any standing aloft and unfolded on
    a bough
Like other flowers, in a revelation of petals;
Silver-pink peach, venetian glass of medlars and
    sorb-apples,
Shallow wine-cups on short, bulging stems
Openly pledging heaven:
Here's to the thorn in flower! Here is to Utterance!
The brave, adventurous rosaceae.

Folded upon itself, and secret unutterable,
And milk-sapped, sap that curdles milk and makes
    ricotta,

Sap that smells strange on your fingers, that even
      goats won't taste it;
Folded upon itself, enclosed like any Mohammedan
      woman,
Its nakedness all within-walls, its flowering forever
      unseen,
One small way of access only, and this close-curtained
      from the light;
Fig, fruit of the female mystery, covert and inward,
Mediterranean fruit, with your covert nakedness,
Where everything happens invisible, flowering and
      fertilisation, and fruiting
In the inwardness of your you, that eye will never see
Till it's finished, and you're over-ripe, and you burst to
      give up your ghost.

Till the drop of ripeness exudes,
And the year is over.

That's how the fig dies, showing her crimson through
      the purple slit
Like a wound, the exposure of her secret, on the
      open day.
Like a prostitute, the bursten fig, making a show of
      her secret.
That's how women die too.

The year is fallen over-ripe,
The year of our women.
The year of our women is fallen over-ripe.
The secret is laid bare.
And rottenness soon sets in.
The year of our women is fallen over-ripe.

When Eve once knew *in her mind* that she was naked
She quickly sewed fig-leaves, and sewed the same for
    the man.
She'd been naked all her days before,
But till then, till that apple of knowledge, she hadn't
    had the fact on her mind.

She got the fact on her mind, and quickly sewed
    fig-leaves.
And women have been sewing ever since.
But now they stitch to adorn the bursten fig, not to
    cover it.
They have their nakedness more than ever on
    their mind,
And they won't let us forget it.
Now, the secret
Becomes an affirmation through moist, scarlet lips
That laugh at the Lord's indignation.

What then, good Lord! cry the women.
We have kept our secret long enough
We are a ripe fig.
Let us burst into affirmation.

They forget, ripe figs won't keep.
Ripe figs won't keep.

Honey-white figs of the north, black figs with scarlet
     inside, of the south.
Ripe figs won't keep, won't keep in any clime.
What then, when women the world over have all
     bursten into self-assertion?
And bursten figs won't keep?

D. H. LAWRENCE

MOON MILK

A ray is caught in a bowl,
And the cat licks it, thinking that it's milk;
Another threads its way through tree-branches,
And the elephant thinks he has found a lotus-stalk.
Half asleep, a girl reaches out
And tries to rearrange the moonbeams on the bed
To share the warmth.
   It is the moon that is drunk with its own light,
   But the world that is confused.

SINCE

On a mid-December day,
frying sausages
for myself, I abruptly
felt under fingers
thirty years younger the rim
of a steering-wheel,
on my cheek the parching wind
of an August noon,
as passenger beside me
You as then you were.

Slap across a veg-growing
alluvial plain
we raced in clouds of white dust,
and geese fled screaming
as we missed them by inches,
making a bee-line
for mountains gradually
enlarging eastward,
joyfully certain nightfall
would occasion joy.

It did. In a flagged kitchen
we were served broiled trout
and a rank cheese: for a while
we talked by the fire,

then, carrying candles, climbed
steep stairs. Love was made
then and there: so halcyoned,
soon we fell asleep
to the sound of a river
swabbling through a gorge.

Since then, other enchantments
have blazed and faded,
enemies changed their address,
and War made ugly
an uncountable number
of unknown neighbors,
precious as us to themselves:
but round your image
there is no fog, and the Earth
can still astonish.

Of what, then, should I complain,
pottering about
a neat suburban kitchen?
Solitude? Rubbish!
It's social enough with real
faces and landscapes
for whose friendly countenance
I at least can learn
to live with obesity
and a little fame.

ELEGIES I.4

Thy husband to a banquet goes with me,
Pray God it may his latest supper be,
Shall I sit gazing as a bashfull guest,
While others touch the damsell I love best?
Wilt lying under him his bosome clippe?
About thy neck shall he at pleasure skippe?
Marveile not though the faire Bride did incite
The drunken *Centaures* to a sodaine fight.
I am no halfe horse, nor in woods I dwell,
Yet scarse my hands from thee containe I well.
But how thou shouldst behave thy selfe now know;
Nor let the windes away my warnings blowe.
Before thy husband come, though I not see
What may be done, yet there before him bee.
Lie with him gently, when his limbes he spread
Upon the bed, but on my foote first tread.
View me, my becks, and speaking countenance:
Take, and receive each secret amorous glaunce.
Words without voyce shall on my eye browes sit,
Lines thou shalt read in wine by my hand writ.
When our lascivious toyes come in thy minde,
Thy Rosie cheekes be to thy thombe inclinde.
If ought of me thou speak'st in inward thought,
Let thy soft finger to thy eare be brought.
When I (my light) do or say ought that please thee,

Turne round thy gold-ring, ass it were to ease thee.
Strike on the boord like them that pray for evill,
When thou doest wish thy husband at the devill.
What wine he fills thee, wisely will him drinke,
Aske thou the boy, what thou enough doest thinke.
When thou hast tasted, I will take the cup,
And where thou drinkst, on that part I will sup.
If hee gives thee what first himselfe did tast,
Even in his face his offered Gobbets cast.
Let not thy necke by his vile armes be prest,
Nor leane thy soft head on his boistrous brest.
Thy bosomes Roseat buds let him not finger,
Chiefely on thy lips let not his lips linger.
If thou givest kisses, I shall all disclose,
Say they are mine, and hands on thee impose.
Yet this Ile see, but if thy gowne ought cover,
Suspitious feare in all my veines will hover,
Mingle not thighes, nor to his legge joyne thine,
Nor thy soft foote with his hard foote combine.
I have beene wanton, therefore am perplext,
And with mistrust of the like measure vext.
I and my wench oft under clothes did lurke,
When pleasure mov'd us to our sweetest worke.
Do not thou so, but throw thy mantle hence,
Least I should thinke thee guilty of offence.
Entreat thy husband drinke, but do not kisse,
And while he drinkes, to adde more do not misse,

If hee lyes downe with Wine and sleepe opprest,
The thing and place shall counsell us the rest.
When to go homewards we rise all along,
Have care to walke in middle of the throng.
There will I finde thee, or be found by thee,
There touch what ever thou canst touch of mee.
Aye me I warne what profits some few howers,
But we must part, when heav'n with black night
         lowers.
At night thy husband clippes thee, I will weepe
And to the dores sight of thy selfe will keepe:
Then will he kisse thee, and not onely kisse
But force thee give him my stolne honey blisse.
Constrain'd against thy will give it the pezant,
Forbeare sweet wordes, and be your sport unpleasant.
To him I pray it no delight may bring,
Or if it do, to thee no joy thence spring:
But though this night thy fortune be to trie it,
To me to morrow constantly deny it.

From DON JUAN

She knew that the best feelings must have victual,
    And that a shipwreck'd youth would hungry be;
Besides, being less in love, she yawn'd a little,
    And felt her veins chill'd by the neighbouring sea;
And so, she cook'd their breakfast to a tittle;
    I can't say that she gave them any tea,
But there were eggs, fruit, coffee, bread, fish, honey,
With Scio wine, – and all for love, not money.

And Zoe, when the eggs were ready, and
    The coffee made, would fain have waken'd Juan;
But Haidee stopp'd her with her quick small hand,
    And without word, a sign her finger drew on
Her lip, which Zoe needs must understand;
    And, the first breakfast spoilt, prepared a new one,
Because her mistress would not let her break
That sleep which seem'd as it would ne'er awake.

AN INVITATION TO AN INVITATION

Hypsithilla, ask me over
Before the week is out, for lunch;
Pity, please, your panting lover
Who wants your goodies in one bunch.
My lovely vixen, please be kind –
Don't have your servant throw me out;
But lay a lovely spread; you'll find
What lays and spreads are all about.
For frankly, it's not food alone
That I am lusting, raging for;
We'll eat, then I'll throw *you* a bone –
And then I'll throw you eight times more.
Ah, love, don't put me off; don't try –
I'm so anxious to begin it;
I think of you, and mercy! my
Tunic's got a tent-pole in it.

CATULLUS   167
TRANS. GARDNER E. LEWIS

SYLVIA

Were I invited to a nectar feast
In heaven, and Venus named me for her guest;
Though Mercury the messenger should prove,
Or her own son, the mighty God of Love;
At the same instant let but honest Tom
From Sylvia's dear terrestrial lodging come,
With look important say – *desires – at three*
Alone – your company – to drink some tea:
Though Tom were mortal, Mercury divine,
Though Sylvia gave me water, Venus wine,
Though heaven was here, and Bow Street lay as far
As the vast distance of the utmost star;
To Sylvia's arms with all my strength I'd fly,
Let who would meet the beauty of the sky.

EPICUREAN REMINISCENCES OF
A SENTIMENTALIST

'My Tables! Meat It Is, I set it down!' – HAMLET.

I think it was Spring – but not certain I am –
    When my passion began first to work;
But I know we were certainly looking for lamb,
    And the season was over for pork.

T'was at Christmas, I think, when I met with Miss —.
    Yes, – for Morris had asked me to dine, –
And I thought I had never beheld such a face,
    Or so noble a turkey and chine.

Placed close by her side, it made others quite wild
    With sheer envy to witness my luck;
How she blushed as I gave her some turtle, and smiled
    As I afterwards offered some duck.

I looked and I languished, alas to my cost,
    Through three courses of dishes and meats;
Getting deeper in love – but my heart was quite lost,
    When it came to the trifle and sweets!

With a rent-roll that told of my houses and land,
    To her parents I told my designs –

169

And then to herself I presented my hand,
  With a very fine pottle of pines!

I asked her to have me for weal or for woe,
  And she did not object in the least; –
I can't tell the date – but we married, I know,
  Just in time to have game at the feast.

We went to —, it certainly was the sea-side;
  For the next, the most blessed of morns,
I remember how fondly I gazed at my bride,
  Sitting down to a plateful of prawns.

O never may memory lose sight of that year,
  But still hallow the time as it ought!
That season the 'grass' was remarkably dear,
  And the peas at a guinea a quart.

So happy, like hours, all our days seemed to haste.
  A fond pair, such as poets have drawn,
So united in heart – so congenial in taste –
  We were both of us partial to brawn!

A long life I looked for of bliss with my bride,
  But then Death – I ne'er dreamt about that!
O, there's nothing is certain in life, as I cried
  When my turbot eloped with the cat!

My dearest took ill at the turn of the year,
    But the cause no physician could nab;
But something it seemed like consumption, I fear, –
    It was just after supping on crab.

In vain she was doctored, in vain she was dosed,
    Still her strength and her appetite pined;
She lost relish for what she had relished the most,
    Even salmon she deeply declined!

For months still I lingered in hope and in doubt,
    While her form it grew wasted and thin;
But the last dying spark of existence went out,
    As the oysters were just coming in!

She died, and she left me the saddest of men,
    To indulge in a widower's moan;
O, I felt all the power of solitude then,
    As I ate my first natives alone!

AT TEA

The kettle descants in a cosy drone,
And the young wife looks in her husband's face,
And then at her guest's, and shows in her own
Her sense that she fills an envied place;
And the visiting lady is all abloom,
And says there was never so sweet a room.

And the happy young housewife does not know
That the woman beside her was first his choice,
Till the fates ordained it could not be so. . . .
Betraying nothing in look or voice
The guest sits smiling and sips her tea,
And he throws her a stray glance yearningly.

IN PRAISE OF COCOA, CUPID'S NIGHTCAP

Lines written upon hearing the startling news
that cocoa is, in fact, a mild aphrodisiac.

Half past nine – high time for supper;
'Cocoa, love?' 'Of course, my dear.'
Helen thinks it quite delicious,
John prefers it now to beer.
Knocking back the sepia potion,
Hubby winks, says, 'Who's for bed?'
'Shan't be long,' says Helen softly,
Cheeks a faintly flushing red.
For they've stumbled on the secret
Of a love that never wanes,
Rapt beneath the tumbled bedclothes,
Cocoa coursing through their veins.

STANLEY J. SHARPLESS

OYSTERS

Charming Oysters I cry,
My Masters come buy,
So plump and so fresh,
So sweet is their Flesh,
 No *Colchester* Oyster,
 Is sweeter and moyster,
 Your Stomach they settle,
 And rouse up your Mettle,
 They'll make you a Dad
 Of a Lass or a Lad;
 And, Madam your Wife
 They'll please to the Life;
Be she barren, be she old,
Be she Slut, or be she Scold,
Eat my Oysters, and lye near her,
She'll be fruitful, never fear her.

FEASTING AND
FASTING

THAT LITTLE OLD BAR IN THE RITZ

When the day's business battle is won,
And your spirits have sunk with the sun,
And again you're aware
That it's time to prepare
For that dinner that's got to be done,
There's a place in the center of town
That can give the required benefits.
So if lacking in pep,
I advise you to step
To that little old bar in the Ritz.

There, Americans, Germans and Greeks
Mix with Arab and Argentine sheiks.
There's a man on one bench
Who's undoubtedly French,
For the waiters all blush when he speaks.
There, where fizzes and punches and grogs
Mix with cocktails and Pommery splits,
International thirst
Can be seen at its worst
At that little old bar in the Ritz.

When your heart has been broken in two,
And you're battered, embittered and blue,
Or when weary you get

Of the same cinq à sept,
And you haven't another in view,
You will find, once you get to this spot,
Far away from the chatter of chits,
You'll thank God that you're male
As you cling to the rail
Of that little old bar in the Ritz.

COLE PORTER

MEAT WITHOUT MIRTH

Eaten I have; and though I had good cheer,
I did not sup, because no friends were there.
Where mirth and friends are absent when we dine
Or sup, there wants the incense and the wine.

THE PARTY'S GOING WITH A SWING

There's something about a family rout
That thrills us,
We like to observe our elders on the sly.
We have to repress the urge to laugh which nearly
      kills us
But nevertheless we try,
Observing every action
And recording every clue
We notice with satisfaction
What some claret cup can do.
The stately advance
Of uncles and aunts
In dozens
Is something to be remembered till we die.
It's often a strain to be polite to all our cousins
But nevertheless we try.
When gossiping and scandal has the party in its grip
The only way to handle it is just to let it rip.

The party's going with a swing, with a swing,
Gay abandon seems to be the thing.
We can say sincerely
That it's really really really
Very pretty to see our elders have an adolescent fling.
Dear old Mrs Giles

Having driven thirty miles
Has an appetite that wouldn't shame a horse,
Having tucked away
Nearly all the cold buffet
She shows every inclination that she's going
      to stay the course.
We're all so glad that Cousin Maud,
Thank the Lord,
Hasn't yet been prevailed upon to sing.
Though dear Miss Scobie's principles forbid her
      to carouse
She's apt to get flirtatious when the atmosphere allows
But it's hard to be seductive when there's junket on
      your blouse.
The party's going with a swing.

The party's going with a swing, with a swing.
Mrs Drew quite took away our breath,
She remarked with candour
Sitting out on the verandah
That as far as she knew old Mr Drew had drunk
      himself to death.
Pretty Mrs Bowles
Having had five sausage rolls
Was compelled to leave the ball room at a bound.
Also Colonel Blake,
Rather gay on tipsy cake,

Emitted first a hiccup then a more peculiar sound.
We can't say what the Vicar did,
God forbid,
But we can blame the moonlight and the Spring,
With hearty joviality he started playing 'Bears',
He pounced on Mrs Frobisher and took her unawares,
We had to cut her laces at the bottom of the stairs.
The party's going with a swing.

The party's going with a swing, with a swing,
All the old folks hand in hand with youth.
Mrs John Macmallard
Bit an almond in the salad
Which completely removed the stopping from her
     one remaining tooth.
Dear old Mrs Spears
Who's been mad for several years
And believes she has the gift of second sight
Went into a trance
Just before the supper dance
And let loose a flood of language which was
     highly impolite.
We're glad Aunt May who's deaf and dumb
Couldn't come
For she does put a blight on everything.
When Mrs Edward Pratt arrived Papa was
     scandalized,

To dance in her condition is a little ill-advised,
If we get her through the Lancers we'll be very much
   surprised.
The party's going with a swing.
Mrs Rogers did some conjuring which held us all in
   thrall,
She cleverly produced a lot of rabbits from her shawl!
But after that the rabbits did the neatest trick of all.
The party's going with a swing.

From THE FUDGE FAMILY IN PARIS

BOOK THREE

DICK, DICK, what a place is this Paris! – but stay –
As my raptures may bore you, I'll just sketch a Day,
As we pass it, myself and some comrades I've got,
All thorough-bred *Gnostics*, who know what is what.

After dreaming some hours of the land of Cockaigne,
    That Elysium of all that is *friand* and nice,
Where for hail they have *bon-bons*, and claret for rain,
    And the skaters in winter show off on *cream-ice*;
Where so ready all nature its cookery yields,
Macaroni au parmesan grows in the fields;
Little birds fly about with the true pheasant taint,
And the geese are all born with a liver complaint!
I rise – put on neck-cloth – stiff, tight, as can be –
For a lad who *goes into the world*, DICK, like me,
Should have his neck tied up, you know – there's no
        doubt of it –
Almost as tight as *some* lads who *go out of it.*
With whiskers well oil'd, and with boots that 'hold up
The mirror to nature' – so bright you could sup
Off the leather like china; with coat, too, that draws
On the tailor, who suffers, a martyr's applause! –
With head bridled up, like a four-in-hand leader,
And stays – devil's in them – too tight for a feeder,

I strut to the old Café Hardy, which yet
Beats the field at a *déjeuner à la fourchette*.
There, DICK, what a breakfast! – oh, not like
    your ghost
Of a breakfast in England, your curst tea and toast;
But a side-board, you dog, where one's eye roves about,
Like a Turk's in the Haram, and thence singles out
One's *pâté* of larks, just to tune up the throat,
One's small limbs of chickens, done *en papillote*,
One's erudite cutlets, drest all ways but plain,
Or one's kidneys – imagine, DICK – done with
    champagne!
Then, some glasses of *Beaune*, to dilute – or, mayhap,
Chambertin, which you know's the pet tipple of NAP,
And which Dad, by the by, that legitimate stickler,
Much scruples to taste, but I'm not so partic'lar. –
Your coffee comes next, by prescription: and then,
    DICK, 's
The coffee's ne'er-failing and glorious appendix –
(If books had but such, my old Grecian, depend on't
I'd swallow even W–tk–n's, for sake of the end on't) –
A neat glass of *parfait-amour*, which one sips
Just as if bottled velvet tipp'd over one's lips.

From SIR GAWAIN AND
THE GREEN KNIGHT

This king lay at Camelot at Christmastide;
Many good knights and gay his guests were there,
Arrayed of the Round Table rightful brothers,
With feasting and fellowship and carefree mirth.
There true men contended in tournaments many,
Joined there in jousting these gentle knights,
Then came to the court for carol-dancing,
For the feast was in force full fifteen days,
With all the meat and the mirth that men could devise,
Such gaiety and glee, glorious to hear,
Brave din by day, dancing by night.
High were their hearts in halls and chambers,
These lords and these ladies, for life was sweet.
In peerless pleasures passed they their days,
The most noble knights known under Christ,
And the loveliest ladies that lived on earth ever,
And he the comeliest king, that that court holds,
For all this fair folk in their first age
                    were still.
          Happiest of mortal kind,
          King noblest famed of will;
          You would now go far to find
          So hardy a host on hill.

While the New Year was new, but yesternight come,
This fair folk at feast two-fold was served,
When the king and his company were come in together,
The chanting in chapel achieved and ended.
Clerics and all the court acclaimed the glad season,
Cried Noel anew, good news to men;
Then gallants gather gaily, hand-gifts to make,
Called them out clearly, claimed them by hand,
Bickered long and busily about those gifts.
Ladies laughed aloud, though losers they were,
And he that won was not angered, as well you will know.
All this mirth they made until meat was served;
When they had washed them worthily, they went to
    their seats,
The best seated above, as best it beseemed,
Guenevere the goodly queen gay in the midst
On a dais well-decked and duly arrayed
With costly silk curtains, a canopy over,
Of Toulouse and Turkestan tapestries rich,
All broidered and bordered with the best gems
Ever brought into Britain, with bright pennies
          to pay.
        Fair queen, without a flaw,
        She glanced with eyes of grey.
        A seemlier that once he saw,
        In truth, no man could say.

But Arthur would not eat till all were served;
So light was his lordly heart, and a little boyish;
His life he liked lively – the less he cared
To be lying for long, or long to sit,
So busy his young blood, his brain so wild.
And also a point of pride pricked him in heart,
For he nobly had willed, he would never eat
On so high a holiday, till he had heard first
Of some fair feat or fray some far-borne tale,
Of some marvel of might, that he might trust,
By champions of chivalry achieved in arms,
Or some suppliant came seeking some single knight
To join with him in jousting, in jeopardy each
To lay life for life, and leave it to fortune
To afford him on field fair hap or other.
Such is the king's custom, when his court he holds
At each far-famed feast amid his fair host
                    so dear.
            The stout king stands in state
            Till a wonder shall appear;
            He leads, with heart elate,
            High mirth in the New Year.

So he stands there in state, the stout young king,
Talking before the high table of trifles fair.
There Gawain the good knight by Guenevere sits,
With Agravain à la dure main on her other side,

Both knights of renown, and nephews of the king.
Bishop Baldwin above begins the table,
And Yvain, son of Urien, ate with him there.
These few with the fair queen were fittingly served;
At the side-tables sat many stalwart knights.
Then the first course comes, with clamor of trumpets
That were bravely bedecked with bannerets bright,
With noise of new drums and the noble pipes.
Wild were the warbles that wakened that day
In strains that stirred many strong men's hearts.
There dainties were dealt out, dishes rare,
Choice fare to choose, on chargers so many
That scarce was there space to set before the people
The service of silver, with sundry meats,
                              on cloth.
                    Each fair guest freely there
                    Partakes, and nothing loth;
                    Twelve dishes before each pair;
                    Good beer and bright wine both.

TRANS. MARIE BORROFF

SONNET TO VAUXHALL

'The English Garden.' MASON

The cold transparent ham is on my fork –
It hardly rains – and hark the bell! – ding-dingle –
Away! Three thousand feet at gravel work,
Mocking a Vauxhall shower! – Married and Single
Crush – rush; – Soaked Silks with wet white Satin
    mingle;
Hengler! Madame! round whom all bright sparks lurk,
Calls audibly on Mr and Mrs Pringle
To study the Sublime, &c. – (vide Burke)
All Noses are upturned! – Wish – ish! – On high
The rocket rushes – trails – just steals in sight –
Then droops and melts in bubbles of blue light –
And Darkness reigns – Then balls flare up and die –
 Wheels whiz – smack crackers – serpents twist –
    and then
Back to the cold transparent ham again!

HENRY KING

WHO CHEWED BITS OF STRING, AND WAS
EARLY CUT OFF IN DREADFUL AGONIES

The Chief Defect of Henry King
    Was chewing little bits of String.
At last he swallowed some which tied
    Itself in ugly Knots inside.
Physicians of the Utmost Fame
Were called at once; but when they came
They answered, as they took their Fees,
'There is no Cure for this Disease.
Henry will very soon be dead.'
His Parents stood about his Bed
Lamenting his Untimely Death,
When Henry, with his Latest Breath,
Cried – 'Oh, my Friends, be warned by me,
That Breakfast, Dinner, Lunch, and Tea
Are all the Human Frame requires . . .'
With that, the Wretched Child expires.

ON THE GREAT EATER OF GRAYS-INN

Oh! for a lasting wind! that I may rail
At this vile Cormorant, this Harpey-male:
That can, with such an hungry haste, devour
A year's provision in one short liv'd hour.
Prodigious calf of Pharaoh's lean-rib'd kine,
That swallowest beef, at every bit a chine!
Yet art thyself so meagre, men may see
Approaching famine in thy phys'nomy.

The World may yet rejoice, thou wer't not one
That shar'd Jove's mercy with Deucalion;
Had he thy grinders trusted in that boat,
Where the whole world's epitome did float,
Clean, and unclean had died, th' Earth found a want
Of her irrational inhabitant:
'Tis doubted, there thy fury had not ceast,
But of the human part too made a feast;

How fruitless then had been Heaven's charity?
No man on earth had liv'd, nor beast, but thee.
Had'st thou been one to feed upon the fare
Stor'd by old Priam for the Grecian war;
He, and his sons had soon been made a prey,
Troy's ten years siege had lasted but one day;
Or thou might'st have preserv'd them, and at once
Chop'd up Achilles, and his Myrmidons.

Had'st thou been Bael, sure thou had'st sav'd the lives
O' th' cheating priests, their children, and their wives,
But at this rate, 'twould be a heavy tax
For Hercules himself to cleanse thy jakes.
Oh! that kind Heav'n to give to thee would please
An Estridge-maw for then we should have peace.
Swords then, or shining engines would be none,
No guns, to thunder out destruction:
No rugged shackles would be extant then,
Nor tedious grates, that limit free-born men.
But thy gut-pregnant womb thy paws do fill
With spoils of Nature's good, and not her ill.

'Twas th' Inns of Courts improvidence to own
Thy wolfish carcase for a son o' th' gown;
The danger of thy jaws, they ne'er foresaw;
For, faith! I think thou hast devour'd the Law.
No wonder th' art complain'd of by the rout,
When very curs begin to smell thee out.
The reasons Southwark rings with howlings are,
Because thou rob'st the bulldogs of their share.

Beastly Consumer! not content to eat
The wholesome quarters destin'd for men's meat,
But excrement and all: nor wilt thou bate
One entrail, to inform us of thy Fate:
Which will, I hope, be such an ugly Death,
As hungry beggars, can in cursings breath.

But I have done, my Muse can scold no more,
She to the Bearward's sentence turns thee o'er,
And, since so great 's thy stomach's tyranny,
For writing this, pray God, thou eat not me.

THE GLUTTON

Pray, pity the poor glutton! –
Who yawns the hours away
From breakfast-time to dinner-time,
From dinner-time to tea!

Oh, pity the poor glutton,
Whose appetite is such
That he can never, never, never
Eat too much!

Oh, pity the poor glutton
Whose troubles all begin
In struggling on and on to turn
What's out into what's in.

ON GUT

Gut eats all day, and lechers all the night,
So all his meat he tasteth over, twice:
And, striving so to double his delight,
He makes himself a thoroughfare of vice.
Thus, in his belly, can he change a sin,
Lust it comes out, that gluttony went in.

BEN JONSON

EPIGRAM VIII.23

Because my cook ruined the mutton
I thrashed him. You protested: 'Glutton!
Tyrant! The punishment should fit
The crime – you can't assault a man
For a spoilt dinner.' Yes, I can.
What worse crime can a cook commit?

MARTIAL   195
TRANS. JAMES MICHIE

THE GOURMAND
With profuse and very necessary apologies

He did not wear his swallow tail,
But a simple dinner coat;
For once his spirits seemed to fail,
And his fund of anecdote.
His brow was drawn and damp and pale,
And a lump stood in his throat.

I never saw a person stare,
With looks so dour and blue,
Upon the square of bill of fare
We waiters call the 'M'noo',
And at every dainty mentioned there,
From *entrée* to *ragoût*.

With head bent low and cheeks aglow,
He viewed the groaning board,
For he wondered if the chef would show
The treasures of his hoard,
When a voice behind him whispered low,
'Sherry or 'ock, m'lord?'

Gods! What a tumult rent the air,
As with a frightful oath,
He seized the waiter by the hair,

And cursed him for his sloth;
Then, grumbling like some stricken bear
Angrily answered, 'Both!'

For each man drinks the thing he loves
As tonic, dram, or drug!
Some do it standing, in their gloves,
Some seated, from a jug;
The upper class from thin-stemmed glass,
The masses from a mug.

The wine was slow to bring him woe,
But when the meal was through,
His wild remorse at every course
Each moment wilder grew;
For he who thinks to mix his drinks
Must mix his symptoms too.

Did he regret that tough *noisette*
And the tougher *tournedos,*
The oysters dry, and the game so high,
And the *soufflé* flat and low
Which the *chef* had planned with a heavy hand,
And the waiters served so slow?

Yet each approves the thing he loves,
From caviare to pork;
Some guzzle cheese or new-grown peas,
Like a cormorant or stork;
The poor man's wife employs a knife,
The rich man's mate a fork.

Some gorge forsooth in early youth,
Some wait till they are old;
Some take their fare off earthenware,
And some from polished gold.
The gourmand gnaws in haste because
The plates so soon grow cold.

Some eat too swiftly, some too long,
In restaurant or grill;
Some, when their weak insides go wrong,
Try a post-prandial pill,
For each man eats his fav'rite meats,
Yet each man is not ill.

He does not sicken in his bed,
Through a night of wild unrest,
With a snow-white bandage round his head,
And a poultice on his breast,
'Neath the nightmare weight of the things he ate
And omitted to digest.

I know not whether meals be short
Or whether meals be long;
All that I know of this resort,
Proves that there's something wrong,
And the soup is weak and tastes of port,
And the fish is far too strong.

To dance to flutes, to dance to lutes,
Is a pastime rare and grand;
But to eat of fish, or fowl, or fruits
To a Blue Hungarian Band
Is a thing that suits nor men nor brutes
As the world should understand.

Such music baffles human talk,
And gags each genial guest;
A grill-room orchestra can baulk
All efforts to digest,
Till the chops will not lie still, but walk
All night upon one's chest.

Six times a table here he booked,
Six times he sat and scanned
The list of dishes badly cooked
By the chef's unskilful hand;
And I never saw a man who looked
So wistfully at the band.

He did not swear or tear his hair,
But drank up wine galore,
As though it were some vintage rare
From an old Falernian store;
With open mouth he slaked his drouth,
And loudly called for more.

He was the type that waiters know,
Who simply lives to feed,
Who little cares what food we show
If it be food indeed,
And, when his appetite is low,
Falls back upon his greed.

For each man eats his fav'rite meats,
(Provided by his wife);
Or cheese or chalk, or peas or pork,
(For such, alas! is life!).
The rich man eats them with a fork,
The poor man with a knife.

From PIERS PLOWMAN, PASSUS V

Now Gluttony at least *began* to go to his shriving,
And went casually kirkwards to confess his sins.
   But Betty the Brewster bade him good morning,
And with that asked him whither he was going.
   'To Holy Church,' said he, 'to hear Mass,
And so to get my shrift, and sin no more.'
   'I have good ale here, gossip. Won't you try some,
      Gluttony?'
'Have you anything in your handbag – any hot spices?'
   'I have pepper and peony-seeds and a pound of
      garlic;
Or a farthing's-worth of fennel, since it's a fast-day.'
   So in goes Gluttony, and Great Oaths follows him.
There Cicely the shoemaker sat on the bench,
With Walt the Warrener, and also his wife,
Timmy the Tinker, and two of his 'prentices,
Hicks who hired-out horses, and Hugh the
      needlemaker,
Clarice the Cock Lane Whore, and the clerk of the
      parish,
David the Ditcher, and a dozen others –
A fiddler, a rat-finder, and a Cheapside filth-raker,
Piers the Prelate and his Flemish popsy Parnel,
A rope-maker, a rider, and Rose the dish-seller,
Godfrey of Garlickhithe, and Griffith the Welshman,

And a rabble of rag-sellers. Early in the morning
All welcomed Gluttony gladly, with a gift of good ale.
   Clement the Cobbler threw off his cloak,
And offered it as his forfeit in a game of New Fair;
Hicks the Hackneyman hurled his hood after it,
And asked Betts the Butcher to be his agent.
Then they chose chapmen to value the exchange,
How much extra should be had by him who owned
      the cloak.
   The two hawkers hurried to have the game over
And, whispering in private, they priced the poor
      pennorths,
But declared that they could not, on their consciences,
      agree...
So they asked Robin the Ropemaker into the ring,
Enlisting him as their umpire, to avoid strife;
And between the three of them the business was
      by-and-by settled.
   Hicks the Hostler was to have the cloak
On condition that Clement should stand him a cupful;
And have Hicks's hood, and shake hands on the deal;
And the first who renegued on the arrangement was
      required
To give old Gluttony a gallon of ale.
   So they laughed and they lowered and yelled,
      'Let's have a drink'
And sat there till Evensong, singing now and then,

Till Gluttony had golloped a gallon or more
And his guts began grumbling like two greedy sows.
He pissed four pints in the space of a Pater-noster
And blew the round bugle at his backbone's end
So that all who heard that horn held their noses,
And wished he had bunged it with a bunch of whins.
He could neither stir nor stand without his stick,
And then walked no better than a bar-fiddler's bitch,
Sometimes sideways and sometimes backwards,
His course criss-crossing like a man laying bird-nets.
    And when he drew near the door, his eyes grew dim;
He thrumbled on the threshold, and was thrown to earth.
Clement the Cobbler caught him round the waist
To lift him a little, at least to his knees;
But Gluttony was a burly brute, and a bastard to lift;
And he coughed-up such a caudle into Clement's lap
There is no hound so hungry in the whole of
        Hertfordshire
He'd have lapped-up those leavings, so unlovely they
        smelt.
    At last, with a world of trouble, his wife and his
        wench
Brought him back home and put him to bed.
There, after all his excesses, he became unconscious,
And slept all Saturday, and all Sunday till sunset.
Then he came out of his coma, and wiped his eyes
        clean;

And the first words from his tongue were, 'Who's
    taken my tankard?'
His wife began to upbraid him for his beastly ways,
And Repentance was there also to rebuke him.
    'Evil in word and deed alike has your life been;
Be ashamed of yourself, show it in your speech, and be
    shriven.'
    'Guilty I am,' said Gluttony, 'I grant it freely.
I've transgressed with my tongue I cannot tell how
    often,
Swearing "by God's soul" and "So help me God and
    the saints",
Nine hundred times, when there wasn't any need for it.
I've stuffed myself so at supper, and sometimes at
    noonday,
That I've spewed it all up along the space of a mile,
Wasting what might have been saved for those in want.
On fast-days I've both drunk and eaten delicacies,
And sometimes been so long at the table that I slept
    while I ate,
Or have taken my meals in taverns, to continue talking
    and tippling;
And even on fast-days have been off to my food before
    noon.'
    'So full a confession cannot fail to win you merit.'
    Then Gluttony began to weep and be in great grief
For the loose life that he had been living;

And he made a vow: 'Every Friday henceforward for ever,
Whatever hunger and thirst I may have,
Not even of fish shall my bowels have knowledge
Till my Auntie Abstinence gives her authority –
She whom till now I've hated all my life!'

WILLIAM LANGLAND
TRANS. TERENCE TILLER

FASTING

There's hidden sweetness in the stomach's emptiness.
We are lutes, no more, no less. If the soundbox
is stuffed full of anything, no music.
If the brain and the belly are burning clean
with fasting, every moment a new song comes out of
      the fire.
The fog clears, and new energy makes you
run up the steps in front of you.
Be emptier and cry like reed instruments cry.
Emptier, write secrets with the reed pen.
When you're full of food and drink, an ugly metal
statue sits where your spirit should. When you fast,
good habits gather like friends who want to help.
Fasting is Solomon's ring. Don't give it
to some illusion and lose your power,
but even if you have, if you've lost all will and control,
they come back when you fast, like soldiers appearing
out of the ground, pennants flying above them.
A table descends to your tents,
Jesus' table.
Expect to see it, when you fast, this table
spread with other food, better than the broth of
      cabbages.

206   RUMI
      TRANS. COLEMAN BARKS

THE GRAPE CURE

For two days feed on water. The third morning
Drink water and eat, some twenty minutes after,
The first of your grapes. In as many weeks as you need
You shall be cured. What happens, in plain words,
Is a purging, a starving not of yourself but of what
Feeds on you, hangs down like a crab from your heart.

The first days have a tang: in a bone cup
Wild honey, locusts, the gracile hermit's lunch,
And goglets cooling among walls; the verb
Of Handel in a starlit attic sounding
The question of how much one ever needs
– Which is high naughtiness in a grave man.

And the ruddy colossus who had guarded you
Moves to a pillar above those crawling sands
In which his absence plants the splendor plucked
By late visitors to that place. And only then,
With the last illusion that anything matters lost
Like a bad penny, do such languors come

That, pulled two ways at once by the distant star
Called Plenitude and the bald planet Ebb,
Your body learns how it is chained to fear.
You learn you need one thing alone which, pressed

Against your palate, is not yet joy, nor even
The hope of it. Your body is like a coast

At sunset, whose morbid flats, the blacks and beggars
Straggling with their hideouts on their backs,
Burn like the cities of antiquity caught
For once without the patina of time;
And at full tide, though winsome, still suspect,
Laid on too thick, but (though suspect) held dear

Lest everything fail: lest after Handel stopped
The listening beasts had not lain down appeased:
Or lest, tomorrow morning, when the sun
Bestrides the vineyards, a sick man should pretend
Somehow that of this chryselephantine air
The gold cannot be pity, nor ivory charity.

CURL UP AND DIET

Some ladies smoke too much and some ladies drink too
 much and some ladies pray too much,
But all ladies think that they weigh too much.
They may be as slender as a sylph or a dryad,
But just let them get on the scales and they embark on
 a doleful jeremiad;
No matter how low the figure the needle happens to
 touch,
They always claim it is at least five pounds too much;
To the world she may appear slinky and feline,
But she inspects herself in the mirror and cries Oh,
 I look like a sea lion.
Yes, she tells you she is growing into the shape of a sea
 cow or manatee,
And if you say No, my dear, she says you are just lying
 to make her feel better, and if you say Yes, my
 dear, you injure her vanity.
Once upon a time there was a girl more beautiful and
 witty and charming than tongue can tell,
And she is now a dangerous raving maniac in a padded
 cell,
And the first indication her friends and relatives had
 that she was mentally overwrought
Was one day when she said, I weigh a hundred and
 twenty-seven, which is exactly what I ought.

Oh, often I am haunted

By the thought that somebody might someday discover
a diet that would let ladies reduce just as much as
they wanted,

Because I wonder if there is a woman in the world
strong-minded enough to shed ten pounds or
twenty,

And say There now, that's plenty;

And I fear me one ten-pound loss would only arouse
the craving for another.

So it wouldn't do any good for ladies to get their
ambition and look like somebody's fourteen-year-
old brother,

Because, having accomplished this with ease,

They would next want to look like somebody's
fourteen-year-old brother in the final stages of
some obscure disease,

And the more success you have the more you want to
get of it,

So then their goal would be to look like somebody's
fourteen-year-old brother's ghost, or rather not
the ghost itself, which is fairly solid, but a
silhouette of it,

So I think it is very nice for ladies to be lithe and
lissome,

But not so much so that you cut yourself if you happen
to embrace or kissome.

ON A DIET

> *Eat all you want*
> *but don't swallow it.*
> ARCHIE MOORE

The ruth of soups and balm of sauces
I renounce equally. What Rorschach saw
in ink I find in the buttery frizzle
in the sauté pan, and I leave it behind,
and the sweet peat-smoke tang of bananas,
and cream in clots, and chocolate. I give
away the satisfactions of food and take
desire for food: I'll be travelling light

to the heaven of revisions. Why be
adipose: an expense, etc.
in a waste, etc.? Something like
the body of the poet's work, with its
pale shadows, begins to pare and replace
the poet's body, and isn't it time?

WILLIAM MATTHEWS   211

LIQUOR IS QUICKER

THE FIVE REASONS

If all be true that I do think,
There are *Five Reasons* we should drink;
Good Wine, a Friend, or being Dry,
Or lest we should be by and by;
Or any other Reason why.

HENRY ALDRICH

REFLECTION ON
ICE-BREAKING

Candy
Is dandy
But liquor
Is quicker.

DRINKING

The thirsty *Earth* soaks up the *Rain*,
And drinks, and gapes for drink again.
The *Plants* suck in the *Earth*, and are
With constant drinking fresh and faire.
The *Sea* it self, which one would think
Should have but little need of *Drink*,
Drinks ten thousand *Rivers* up,
So fill'd that they oreflow the *Cup*.
The busie *Sun* (and one would guess
By's drunken fiery face no less)
Drinks up the *Sea*, and when h'as done,
The *Moon* and *Stars* drink up the *Sun*.
They drink and dance by their own light,
They drink and revel all the night.
Nothing in *Nature's Sober* found,
But an eternal *Health* goes round.
Fill up the *Bowl*, then fill it high,
Fill all the *Glasses* there, For why
Should every creature drink but *I*,
Why, *Man* of *Morals*, tell me why?

FACING WINE

Never refuse wine. I'm telling you,
people come smiling in spring winds:

peach and plum like old friends, their
open blossoms scattering toward me,

singing orioles in jade-green trees,
and moonlight probing gold winejars.

Yesterday we were flush with youth,
and today, white hair's an onslaught.

Bramble's overgrown Shih-hu Temple,
and deer roam Ku-su Terrace ruins:

it's always been like this, yellow dust
choking even imperial gates closed

in the end. If you don't drink wine,
where are those ancient people now?

LI PO   217
TRANS. DAVID HINTON

ON ONE, WHO SAID, HE DRANK TO CLEAR HIS EYES

As Phoebus, crawling to his Western seat,
His shining face bedew'd with beamy sweat,
His flaming eyes at last grown blood-shot red,
By atoms sprung from his hot horses' speed,
Drives to that sea-green bosom of his Love's,
And in her lap his fainting light improves;

So Thyrsis, when at th' unresisted flame
Of thy fair Mistress's eye, thine dull became,
In sovereign sack thou did'st an eye-salve seek,
And stol'st a blest dew from her rosy cheek:
When straight thy lids a cheerful vigour wore,
More quick and penetrating than before.

I saw the sprightly grape in glory rise,
And with her day thy drooping night surprise,
So that, where now a giddy darkness dwells,
Brightness now breaks through liquid spectacles.

Had Adam known this cure in Paradise,
He'd scap'd the Tree, and drunk to clear his eyes.

CONSUMMATE DRINKERS

To you, consummate drinkers,
    Though little be your drought,
Good speed be to your tankards,
    And send the wine about.
Let not the full decanter
    Sleep on its round,
And may unheard-of banter
    In wit abound.

If any cannot carry
    His liquor as he should,
Let him no longer tarry,
    No place here for the prude.
No room among the happy
    For modesty.
A fashion only fit for clowns,
    Sobriety.

If such by chance are lurking
    Let them be shown the door;
He who good wine is shirking,
    Is one of us no more.
A death's head is his face to us,
    If he abide.
Who cannot keep the pace with us,
    As well he died.

Should any take upon him
    To drink without a peer,
Although his legs go from him,
    His speech no longer clear,
Still for his reputation
    Let him drink on,
And swig for his salvation
    The bumper down.

But between god and goddess,
    Let there no marriage be,
For he whose name is Liber
    Exults in liberty.
Let none his single virtue
    Adulterate,
Wine that is wed with water is
    Emasculate.

Queen of the sea we grant her,
    Goddess without demur,
But to be bride to Bacchus
    Is not for such as her.
For Bacchus drinking water
    Hath no man seen;
Nor ever hath his godship
    Baptized been.

ODES III.21

Wine-jar whose birth-year, Manlius' consulship,
Was mine as well, unstopper of elegies,
    Jokes, quarrels, love's crazed fits, and blessed
        Effortless slumber (your kindest office),

You've kept the choice old Massic in store for a
Great moment: now, whatever occasion you
    Foresaw, descend like Jove – my guest has
        Called for a mellower wine from upstairs.

His drink is Plato's wisdom of Socrates –
Deep tipple; yet he'll never uncivilly
    Snub *you*: they say old Cato often
        Warmed his morale with an undiluted

Cup. Jar, you put brains stolid by nature to
Torment on your sweet rack; the philosopher's
    Dark thoughts are bared, most secret counsels
        Spilled at the prompting of jolly Bacchus;

You rally lost hopes back to the worry-worn,
You bring the poor man courage and confidence:
    Crowned kings can rage, call out their soldiers –
        After a taste of you, he'll defy them.

Friends keep you up late: Liber with Venus, when
She's gay, the three linked Graces who hate to let
    Go hands, and bright lamps burning on till
        Phoebus, returning, defeats the starlight.

HORACE
TRANS. JAMES MICHIE

GREAT BACCHUS
from the Greek

Great Bacchus, born in thunder and in fire,
By native heat asserts his dreadful sire.
Nourish'd near shady rills and cooling streams,
He to the nymphs avows his amorous flames.
To all the brethren at the Bell and Vine,
The moral says; mix water with your wine.

DRINKING IN THE MORNING

I don't want to drink in ruins under a sky
    The belly of a wild ass.

Nor under a roof that sieves rain with broken walls
    Which let in great mounds of soil.

I want to drink in the morning when heaven appears
    Wearing a kaftan of voile;

And the Eastern breeze goes for a stroll through a
      garden
    Full of blossom lapped with dew;

And the bright sun is like a newly minted dinar.

ABDULLAH IBN AL-MU'TAZZ   223
TRANS. G. B. H. WIGHTMAN AND
ABDULLAH AL-UDHARI

DRINKING ALONE

As if they could feel, spring grasses
turn shade beside the house jade-green.

When this east wind blows, grief comes.
I sit out in its bluster, my hair white,

and drink alone, inviting my shadow.
Chanting lazily, I face trees in flower.

Old pine, what have you learned? Cold,
cold and desolate – who's your song for?

On stone, fingers in moonlight dance
over the *ch'in* in my lapful of blossoms.

Out beyond this jar of wine, it's all
longing, longing – no heart of mine.

224 LI PO
TRANS. DAVID HINTON

USQUEBAUGH

Deft, practised, eager,
Your fingers twist the metal cap.
Late into the moth-infested night
We listen to soft scrapings
Of bottle-top on ridged glass,

The plash and glug of amber liquid
Streaming into tumblers, inches deep.
Life-water. Fire-tanged
Hard-stuff. Gallons of it,
Sipped and swigged and swallowed.

Whiskey: its terse vowels belie
The slow fuddling and mellowing,
Our guttural speech slurring
Into warm, thick blather,
The pie-eyed, slug-witted slump

Into soused oblivion –
And the awakening. I long
For pure, cold water as the pump
Creaks in the yard. A bucket
Clatters to the ground. Is agony.

WENDY COPE   225

HOGMANAY

Murdo gave the cock meal
damped with whisky. It stood
on tiptoe, crowed eight times
and fell flat on its beak.

Later, Murdo, after the fifth verse
of *The Isle of Mull*,
fell, glass in hand,
flat on his back – doing in six hours
what the cock had done
in two minutes.

I was there. And now I see
the cock crowing with Murdo's face
and Murdo's wings flapping
as down he went.

It was a long way home.

JOHN BARLEYCORN

A BALLAD

There were three kings into the east,
   Three kings both great and high,
An' they ha'e sworn a solemn oath
   John Barleycorn should die.

They took a plough and ploughed him down,
   Put clods upon his head,
An' they ha'e sworn a solemn oath
   John Barleycorn was dead.

But the cheerful spring came kindly on,
   And showers began to fall;
John Barleycorn got up again,
   And sore surprised them all.

The sultry suns of summer came,
   And he grew thick and strong,
His head weel armed wi' pointed spears,
   That no one should him wrong.

The sober autumn entered mild,
   When he grew wan and pale;
His bending joints and drooping head
   Showed he began to fail.

His colour sickened more and more,
    He faded into age;
And then his enemies began
    To show their deadly rage.

They 've ta'en a weapon long and sharp,
    And cut him by the knee;
Then tied him fast upon a cart,
    Like a rogue for forgerie.

They laid him down upon his back,
    And cudgelled him full sore;
They hung him up before the storm,
    And turned him o'er and o'er.

They fillèd up a darksome pit
    With water to the brim,
They heavèd in John Barleycorn,
    There let him sink or swim.

They laid him out upon the floor,
    To work him farther woe,
And still, as signs of life appeared,
    They tossed him to and fro.

They wasted, o'er a scorching flame,
 The marrow of his bones;
But a miller used him worst of all,
 For he crushed him 'tween two stones.

And they ha'e ta'en his very heart's blood,
 And drank it round and round;
And still the more and more they drank,
 Their joy did more abound.

John Barleycorn was a hero bold,
 Of noble enterprise,
For if you do but taste his blood,
 'Twill make your courage rise.

'Twill make a man forget his woe;
 'Twill heighten all his joy:
'Twill make the widow's heart to sing,
 Though the tear were in her eye.

Then let us toast John Barleycorn,
 Each man a glass in hand;
And may his great posterity
 Ne'er fail in old Scotland!

ROBERT BURNS

THE SOUL OF THE WINE

sang by night in its bottles: 'Dear mankind –
dear and disinherited! Break the seal
of scarlet wax that darkens my glass jail,
and I shall bring you light and brotherhood!

How long you labored on the fiery hills
among the needful vines! I know it cost
fanatic toil to make me what I am,
and I shall not be thankless or malign:

I take a potent pleasure when I pour
down the gullet of a workingman,
and how much more I relish burial
in his hot belly than in my cold vaults!

Listen to my music after hours,
the hope that quickens in my throbbing heart;
lean on the table with your sleeves rolled up
and honor me: you will know happiness,

for I shall bring a gleam to your wife's eyes,
a glow of power to your son's wan cheeks
and for this athlete flagging in the race
shall be the oil that strengthens wrestlers' limbs.

Into you I shall flow, ambrosia brewed
from precious seed the eternal Sower cast,
so that the poetry born of our love will grow
and blossom like a flower in God's sight!'

CHARLES BAUDELAIRE
TRANS. RICHARD HOWARD

WINEJUG

You are the guilty debtor of a long thirst,
the wise procurer of wine and water,
on your sides, the young goats dance
and the fruits ripen to the music.

The flutes whistle, swear and are angry
at the trouble on your black and red rim
and no one can take you up
and put this trouble right.

OSIP MANDELSTAM,   231
TRANS. RICHARD AND ELIZABETH MCKANE

THE WINE OF THE QUESTION

When my Friend lifts a glass in here,
the marketplace suddenly loses customers.

I kneel weeping.
Will you take my hand?

I float like a fish
waiting for your hook.

Most people see your eyes
and call for the police,

but Hafiz knows that the wine you offer
is the wine in the *Qur'an* of the question,
Am I not your Lord?

that you poured
as we said *Yes.*

HIS FAREWELL TO SACK

Farewell thou thing, time past so known, so dear
To me as blood to life and spirit; near,
Nay, thou more near than kindred, friend, man, wife,
Male to the female, soul to body; life
To quick action, or the warm soft side
Of the resigning, yet resisting bride.
The kiss of virgins, first fruits of the bed,
Soft speech, smooth touch, the lips, the maidenhead:
These and a thousand sweets could never be
So near or dear as thou wast once to me.
O thou, the drink of gods and angels! wine
That scatter'st spirit and lust, whose purest shine
More radiant than the summer's sunbeams shows;
Each way illustrious, brave, and like to those
Comets we see by night, whose shagg'd portents
Foretell the coming of some dire events,
Or some full flame which with a pride aspires,
Throwing about his wild and active fires;
'Tis thou, above nectar, O divinest soul!
Eternal in thyself, that can'st control
That which subverts whole nature, grief and care,
Vexation of the mind, and damn'd despair.
'Tis thou alone who, with thy mystic fan,
Work'st more than wisdom, art, or nature can
To rouse the sacred madness and awake

The frost-bound blood and spirits, and to make
Them frantic with thy raptures flashing through
The soul like lightning, and as active too.
'Tis not Apollo can, or those thrice three
Castalian sisters, sing, if wanting thee.
Horace, Anacreon, both had lost their fame,
Had'st thou not fill'd them with thy fire and flame.
Phoebean splendour! and thou, Thespian spring!
Of which sweet swans must drink before they sing
Their true-pac'd numbers and their holy lays,
Which makes them worthy cedar and the bays.
But why, why longer do I gaze upon
Thee with the eye of admiration?
Since I must leave thee, and enforc'd must say
To all thy witching beauties, Go, away.
But if thy whimpering looks do ask me why,
Then know that nature bids thee go, not I.
'Tis her erroneous self has made a brain
Uncapable of such a sovereign
As is thy powerful self. Prithee not smile,
Or smile more inly, lest thy looks beguile
My vows denounc'd in zeal, which thus much show
    thee
That I have sworn but by thy looks to know thee.
Let others drink thee freely, and desire
Thee and their lips espous'd, while I admire
And love thee, but not taste thee. Let my muse

Fail of thy former helps, and only use
Her inadult'rate strength: what's done by me
Hereafter shall smell of the lamp, not thee.

ROBERT HERRICK

A VOICE FROM UNDER THE TABLE
to Robert and Jane Brooks

How shall the wine be drunk, or the woman known?
I take this world for better or for worse,
But seeing rose carafes conceive the sun
My thirst conceives a fierier universe:
And then I toast the birds in the burning trees
That chant their holy lucid drunkenness;
I swallowed all the phosphorus of the seas
Before I fell into this low distress.

You upright people all remember how
Love drove you first to the woods, and there you heard
The loose-mouthed wind complaining *Thou and Thou*;
My gawky limbs were shuddered by the word.
Most of it since was nothing but charades
To spell that hankering out and make an end,
But the softest hands against my shoulder-blades
Only increased the crying of the wind.

For this the goddess rose from the midland sea
And stood above the famous wine-dark wave,
To ease our drouth with clearer mystery
And be a South to all our flights of love.
And down by the selfsame water I have seen
A blazing girl with skin like polished stone

Splashing until a far-out breast of green
Arose and with a rose contagion shone.

'A myrtle-shoot in hand, she danced; her hair
Cast on her back and shoulders a moving shade.'
Was it some hovering light that showed her fair?
Was it of chafing dark that light was made?
Perhaps it was Archilochus' fantasy,
Or that his saying sublimed the thing he said.
All true enough; and true as well that she
Was beautiful, and danced, and is now dead.

Helen was no such high discarnate thought
As men in dry symposia pursue,
But was as bitterly fugitive, not to be caught
By what men's arms in love or fight could do.
Groan in your cell; rape Troy with sword and flame;
The end of thirst exceeds experience.
A devil told me it was all the same
Whether to fail by spirit or by sense.

God keep me a damned fool, nor charitably
Receive me into his shapely resignations.
I am a sort of martyr, as you see,

A horizontal monument to patience.
The calves of waitresses parade about
My helpless head upon this sodden floor.
Well, I am down again, but not yet out.
O sweet frustrations, I shall be back for more.

ACKNOWLEDGMENTS

Thanks are due to the following copyright holders for their permission to reprint:

ABDULLAH IBN AL-MU'TAZZ: 'And the lemon …' and 'I don't want to drink…' from *Birds Through a Ceiling of Alabaster: Three Abbasid Poets* (Arab Poetry of the Abbasid Period), translated by G. B. H. Wightman and A. Y. al-Udhari (Penguin Classics, 1973), copyright © G. B. H. Wightman and A. Y. al-Udhari, 1975. Reproduced by permission of G. B. H. Wightman. W. H. AUDEN: 'In Schrafft's' and 'Since' copyright © 1976 by Edward Mendelson, William Meredith and Monroe K. Spears, Executors of the Estate of W. H. Auden. Used by permission of Random House, Inc. in the US and in the UK by Faber and Faber Ltd. BAUDELAIRE: 'The Soul of the Wine' from *Les Fleurs du Mal* by Charles Baudelaire. Translated by Richard Howard. Translation copyright © 1982 by Richard Howard. Reprinted by permission of David R. Godine, Publisher. HILAIRE BELLOC: 'On Food' and 'Henry King'. Reprinted by permission of PFD on behalf of: The Estate of Hilaire Belloc © The Estate of Hilaire Belloc: as printed in the original volume. ELIZABETH BISHOP: 'A Miracle for Breakfast' from *The Complete Poems: 1927–1979* by Elizabeth Bishop. Copyright © 1979, 1983 by Alice Helen Methfessel. Reprinted by permission of Farrar, Straus and Giroux, LLC. MARIE BORROFF: extract from

241

division of Random House, Inc. and in the UK by permission of Anthony Hecht. RALPH HODGSON: 'The Hever Picnic' from *Collected Poems* by Ralph Hodgson. Reproduced with permission of Palgrave Macmillan. HORACE: Ode III.xxi from *The Odes of Horace*, translated by James Michie (Penguin, 1967). Reprinted by permission of David Higham Associates. RUDYARD KIPLING: 'A Song of Bananas' from *Collected Poems* by Rudyard Kipling. Reprinted by permission of A. P. Watt Ltd. on behalf of The National Trust for Places of Historical Interest and Natural Beauty. KRINAGORAS: 'A Simple Feast' translated by Alistair Elliot from *The Greek Anthology and Other Ancient Greek Epigrams*, edited by Peter Jay, Penguin, 1974. © Alistair Elliot. WILLIAM LANGLAND: extract from *Piers Plowman*, translated by Terence Tiller © Terence Tiller, 1981, published by BBC Worldwide Ltd. D. H. LAWRENCE: 'Figs' from *The Complete Poems of D. H. Lawrence*. Reprinted by permission of Pollinger Ltd. and the Estate of Frieda Lawrence Ravagli. LI PO: 'Facing Wine' and 'Drinking Alone' from *The Selected Poems of Li Po* translated by David Hinton. Copyright © 1996 by David Hinton. In the US and Canada, reprinted by permission of New Directions Publishing Corp. In the UK and Commonwealth, published by Anvil Press Poetry in 1996. NORMAN MACCAIG: 'Hogmanay' from *Collected Poems* by Norman MacCaig, published by Chatto and Windus. Reprinted by permission of the Random House

243

INDEX OF AUTHORS

251